LOST IN THE SHUFFLE

The Co-dependent Reality

Robert Subby

Health Communications, Inc.
Deerfield Beach, Florida

Robert Subby, M.A., C.C.D.P.
Licensed Psychologist
Family Systems Center
Edina, Minnesota

Library of Congress Cataloging-in-Publication Data

Subby, Robert, 1949-
    Lost in the shuffle.

    1. Co-dependence (Psychology) — Popular works.
I. Title.
RC569.5.C63S83   1987   616.89   87-8722
ISBN 0-932194-45-1 (pbk.)

© 1987   Health Communications, Inc.
            Enterprise Center
            3201 Southwest 15th Street
            Deerfield Beach, FL 33442

ISBN 0-932194-45-1

All rights reserved. Printed in the United States of America. No part of this publication may be reproduced, stored in a retrieval system or transmitted in any form or by any means, electronic, mechanical, photocopying, recording or otherwise without the written permission of the publisher.

Cover Design and Illustrations by Reta Kaufman.

Acknowledgments

To my loving parents, Walt and Peg, to my brother, Richard, and to my sisters, Pam, Cindy and Candace for the gift of a recovering family.

To the teachers, mentors and friends who have encouraged and supported me along the way.

To Richard Fowler, Ellen Berscheid, Sharon Wegscheider-Cruse, Robert Ackerman, Claudia Black, Vernon Johnson, Frank Kalgren, John Friel, Alcoholics Anonymous and my Higher Power.

Thank you for your love and direction.

Special Acknowledgments

To Mark Worden for his talent, energy and commitment in the organization and editing of *Lost In The Shuffle*. Also to Judy D. for her contribution to this book.

Dedication

To Isabelle Anne Hansen, the love and inspiration of my life.

Preface

On Being Lost In The Shuffle

Who's on first? What's on second? Where am I going? What's the meaning of life . . . and who in the hell am I, anyway?

These are the questions that best described my situation as I faced into the challenges of an adult life. Back then I didn't have the foggiest idea of what being an adult meant. Of course, I thought I did. Being adult naturally meant doing all the things adults did. Simple. At least it seemed simple until I started getting into it.

But it wasn't as simple as I thought, and before long I found myself faking it — faking my way through the labyrinth of adulthood. Inside I felt stupid, inadequate, and afraid of blowing it, afraid of making mistakes and being found out. Even with a college degree in hand and lots of verbal support from friends and family, I felt empty, insecure and alone.

"I shouldn't feel this way," I told myself. "After all, I have it pretty good in comparison to a lot of other folks I know." The pressure to succeed was overwhelming, and despite all the "Right Stuff" I was filled with free-floating anxiety and self-doubt.

The expectations of my family script loomed over me like a dark cloud thundering, "Be a success, make us proud, be happy, be competent, do it right, take care of yourself, be honest, get married, have children, buy a house, be a man and don't be afraid!" What an order!

No doubt a majority of young people feel the anxiety of preparing to break out on their own and face a world which is at best indifferent. But these feelings weren't supposed to last — or so I thought. Unfortunately for me and for millions of other people in similar situations, the anxiety and fear of not making the grade would follow us across decades of adult life with no resolution or relief in sight. The millions I refer to are the millions who came from or who got caught up in troubled family systems, where their ability to grow and develop had been stifled.

For me, the shame and confusion of growing up in an alcoholic family first stood between me and the person I wished to be. The lack I felt inside as a child was destined to be the lack I would feel as an adult.

No trust, no autonomy and no real sense of self — these were the cornerstones of a childhood that never should have happened, but did. The role models I had growing up were all I knew, and these were not models I had any faith in. With no clear model to draw from, I simply got "Lost in the Shuffle."

So this book — *LOST IN THE SHUFFLE* — is written for those who seek to find themselves and break free of a troubled past. Nothing changes until something changes. My hope is that by reading *LOST IN THE SHUFFLE* you will find a beginning for change.

Robert Subby
Bloomington, Minnesota

Contents

PART ONE

Between a Hug
and a Hard Place

Chapter 1

Between a Hug
and a Hard Place

I've been a therapist and a chemical dependency professional for the past 15 years, but, embarrassingly enough, I found my way into the helping field as a practicing alcoholic, adult child, co-dependent. I began my career as a probation officer and case manager for a federally-funded Drunk Driving program in Minneapolis. My primary responsibility in that position was to evaluate and refer people who had been arrested for drunk driving.

My first real job . . .

What a place to begin . . .

There I was, an active alcoholic myself, and I was making decisions about a lot of other alcoholics who, unlike me, had been caught. I was strictly OTL — Out to Lunch. I used to tell myself how lucky I was that *I* was still in control of my drinking.

"I can handle it," I told myself. I wasn't like these alcoholics I was referring to treatment. Sure, I had a drink or two after work, but I wasn't that bad. I was a . . . Social Drinker. And, of course I wasn't nearly as bad as the real alcoholics I knew.

"No problem," I reflected, "I know my limit. I know when to quit. And if I ever feel like my drinking's getting out of control, I'll back off and slow it down."

What a sham! After a tough day of diagnosing the drinking problems of drunk drivers and mandating treatment for many of them (who, needless to say did not want to go to treatment), I would go home and start my evening of "social drinking."

Alone!

And many were the mornings when I went to work with brackish dragon-breath and a raging hangover the Plop Plop Fizz Fizz of Alka Seltzer wouldn't touch. I would get some coffee into my queasy stomach, and then only slightly out of kilter, I would begin making decisions about the lives of folks who had *real* drinking problems.

Like so many of my professional counterparts who found their way into the alcoholism field while they were still drinking, I was sincerely deluded. Sincere delusion is the worst kind of delusion precisely because it is sincere. In other words, I was not in touch at all with my own problem. In fact, I took pride in the idea that I knew what I was doing, and that I was good at recognizing what others were doing.

So with no qualms at all, no misgivings, I continued being the astute professional, judging others and sending them off to treatment for their alcoholism.

I was sending alcoholics to treatment — I mean I knew what I needed, and I certainly knew what they needed. But *I* wasn't ready to go yet, so I sent them in my place. And then I would see them when they came back to see how it went.

Finally, however, there came a point when I could no longer deny that the alcohol problem I saw so often in others was also my own. This recognition came slowly. Like all alcoholics, I didn't want to admit having a problem with alcohol. After all, I was a professional. I could treat myself.

Besides, I thought if I admitted being an alcoholic, I would probably lose my job. Or worse, heaven forbid.

I might have to go to treatment.

"I'm just over-reacting," I told myself. "I can handle it. It's just this job. The pressure. The stress. I need a vacation." And so on. Hope — that is, *Delusion* — springs eternal.

Near the middle of the second year on my job, I "came to." I awoke to the fact that my sincere delusion was not giving me an accurate view of myself. My sincere delusion was falling apart. I couldn't live with my guilt. I felt like a hypocrite.

Good. Because that's what I was — a hypocrite.

Fueled by guilt, I plunged headlong into Alcoholics Anonymous. Of course, in typical fashion I decided to do my recovery quickly and perfectly. In the beginning, I was one of those AA zealots who was just "high on sobriety."

"Piece of cake," I thought in my innocence.

The honeymoon high on sobriety didn't last long. As I came back to earth the pain of my past and the anxiety of all the unfinished business began to surface. Thoughts of drinking filled my head. At any rate, about six months into my pleasure trip of sobriety, while going to all my meetings and doing everything *perfectly,* I was on the verge of falling off the wagon. Just to mention it now, and as we will see later, I was a co-dependent Adult Child of an Alcoholic who had to do everything perfectly.

I was working my program — I was going to all my meetings, even more than I thought I should be going to. I started to feel like I was getting nowhere fast.

AA burnout, I thought.

"No way," the Old Timers said. "Just hang in there." And they repeated the standard slogans.

"One day at a time."

"Let go and let God."

"Don't drink and go to your meetings."

"Read the Big Book."

In other words, I thought, *I'll just have to suffer through. White knuckle it.* Like a lot of other folks, I'd just have to work my program until my bones felt like they were coming through my skin.

So for the next several years I continued hanging in there. And I was not having a Real *Serene* Recovery, if you know what I mean. I was one of those "Damn Happy" alcoholics.

Still, I was determined to do everything *perfectly*. you see, I am an adult child of an alcoholic who had to do everything perfectly.

No one was going to get weller faster than I was. Come hell or high water, I was going to get my Black Belt in AA. Maybe even a third degree Black Belt.

And I was still working as a therapist, "helping" others get well. Needless to say, it was a very difficult period in my recovery, and at times, very awkward. For example, I had lots of anxiety over the fact that many of my clients had more sobriety than I did. Talk about the blind leading the blind.

Even more threatening was the fact that in Minnesota at that time, there was a kind of magical credentialing process: If you had two years of sobriety, then you were considered competent — a legitimate therapist. Degreed or not, the main thing was to be sober longer than your clients.

I remember during those years as an alcoholism counselor working with outpatient clients who started treatment with more sobriety than I had. On top of that, I didn't look very old — I was only 25. Sometimes clients sensed my lack of experience, and they'd ask questions like: "How long have you been sober, Bob?" It was a question I came to dread. It was a threat and a challenge to maintain my composure.

I wasn't stupid. I had studied all the right avenues to escape this kind of interrogation and avoid being pinned down. First I'd look my interrogator right in the eyes, nod gravely, knit my brow and give him my most serious, professional look. Then I'd say, "Now wait just a minute. We are not here to discuss my sobriety. We're here to talk about *your* sobriety."

What a brilliant and professional maneuver, I thought, dodging that question and turning it back on the client who was obviously real sick and screwed up and trying to avoid his own issues.

Having successfully blocked this unsavory line of questioning, I'd finish them off by quoting something out of the *AA Manual of Recovery* according to Bob S. Something like: "We all have the same amount of sobriety — 24 hours." Or: "It isn't the quantity of sobriety that counts, it's the quality." I always kept a bagful of these really useful slogans around just in case some smart-aleck client would try to blindside me.

Despite my Academy Award performances as a "really together guy" I knew I was faking it. Beneath my surface image of okay-ness, was a child who lived in constant fear and anxiety that I would be found out, that someone would see through my act.

On the sixth month of "Real Serene" Recovery, someone in my home AA group had kept track of my sobriety and decided to award me a sixth-month chip for not drinking. God knows, I had been counting the days, but I wasn't up to a celebration about it. In fact, most of what I was thinking about at that point in my sobriety was: When can I start drinking again?

I mean, if this was serenity, who needed it?

How long would it take to get some of that wonderful serenity all those Old Timers in my group were talking about?

When I was just starting out in AA, an Old Timer was anyone over 40. I never planned to live to be 25, much less 40. These old fogies were constantly talking to me as if I were one of their kids. They'd say things like: "Someday, son, you're going to be serene, just work the program." I hated them for not understanding me, and I was real defiant towards anyone who talked to me like that.

So whenever I heard that "Someday, son" business, I'd think, "If I have to wait to be as old as you to have some serenity, well, forget it." I began to think, "Maybe all this serenity stuff is just another name for old age, burnout, fatigue, or exhaustion. Maybe all these 40 year olds weren't really serene after all — just tired and worn out."

Besides, I had taken all their inventories — I knew th. they probably left the meetings and went home to drink.

Ethyl with her red-hennaed hair and magenta lipstick probably went home to sip at those little bottles of vodka the
airlines serve. And Sam — I just knew that he wasn't staying
sober, because he sounded, well, a shade *too* real, he pro-
tested too much. And where do you suppose Leo got those
watery red eyes? And wasn't Janice a devotee of Prince
Valium?

Nope, no way. I knew these people were just *pretending* to
stay sober. Of course my special insight into their behavior
gave me good reason to discount all their sage advice about
"working on my program."

My head was full of these thoughts on the day my group
presented me with my sixth-month sobriety chip. I walked
into that meeting, and I mean to tell you, I was seriously
thinking about getting drunk. I sat down, and all of a sud-
den this woman says, "It's Bob Subby's six-month sobriety."

I thought to myself, six months. Big deal. But then what
else would you expect of a Mickey Mouse organization like
AA? They did little things like birthday parties, and cup-
cakes. Making such a big production about something so
simple and inconsequential as six months of sobriety was
hard for a serious guy like me to swallow.

I said to myself, "Oh my God, they're going to do this to
me!" I tightened up inside. I'd seen them do this number on
other people, and I had been embarrassed for the other
people who got these Mickey Mouse awards. They always
cried and carried on. I was sure they cried only because they
were embarrassed.

"Oh, no, they're doing it to me." First thing, this woman
got all teary-eyed. She was so proud of me, she said, and she
starts saying a lot of stuff I don't remember because my
brain's racing ahead of her trying to find a way to handle the
situation. Up to this point I had been faking recovery real
well. You see, if you're an adult child of an alcoholic like
me, it doesn't take you long to figure out the rules of the
game. You figure out how to look healthy even though
you're sick as hell. You learn to look good, even though

you're scrambling around inside desperately trying to keep yourself together, trying to keep others from learning the horrible truth about you.

After she finished her little speech about my birthday, she walks over and puts this ridiculous little pin on me. I thought, "Oh, God, not one of those dorkey pins."

After I got my dorkey pin, I realized I was supposed to say something to people.

Now I was in trouble. Big trouble. At times like this you're supposed to be healthy enough to say something brilliant and profound. So I scrambled around inside and came up with my "healthy guy" routine, a dialogue I picked up from listening to the Old Timers. "I'm — I'm so grateful to be here," I stammered. "It's wonderful . . . I'm so thankful . . . I'm really proud to be here . . . AA saved my life . . . Six months sobriety, well, what can I say? It's really, uhm, a miracle . . . I couldn't have done it without all of you."

I was trying to work up some tears, but I just couldn't do it. When I cry, I have to have some good reason to cry, and besides, at this point I was too busy scrambling around trying to get out of this creepy situation without humiliating myself beyond redemption. If bullshit was snow, we'd have been in a blizzard.

When I got done with my line of driveling babble, this *big* old truck driver who was in our group stood up. I thought, "Oh God, what's he going to do?" He had a huge beer belly and big varicose veins on his face and nose. A stereotyped kind of drunk if I'd ever seen one. I'd always suspected that he never *really* got sober — he just came to AA because it was a comfortable place to hang out, smoke, and drink coffee.

After he got up, he walked over, stood right in front of me, gave me a crooked smile and rumbled, "Son, I'd like to give you a hug."

A hug! "Oh, shit." My heart sank. I mean this guy was no shining example, no Leo Buscaglia. He had no class, no charisma — unless you count cirrhosis of the liver as a charismatic sign. To me, he was just another one of those AA phonies, and he wanted to give me one of those Mickey Mouse hugs.

Not just a common garden variety hug, either. He wanted to hug me right there in front of all those people.

No man had ever hugged me before. Never! There had always been a lot of hugging at those AA meetings, but I had always managed to avoid the hugs by arriving late and leaving early. Always. "Gotta get going, got an appointment to get to." God forbid that someone should try to hug me at the end of a meeting.

But there I was — trapped. So I said to myself, "What the hell, I'm healthy, I can handle it. No problem." I stood right up and that old truck driver wrapped his long arms around me and stuck his beer gut into me, and gave me a huge AA hug. I can remember going "Oh my God, this guy's . . . *touching* me!"

He hugged me real tight, put his head along side of mine and whispered in my ear, "Son, I think you're full of shit." He didn't say this loud enough for anyone else to hear. He was a neat guy — he wasn't into embarrassing me in front of everybody.

Being the cool, together guy that I was, I just went on acting like he hadn't said anything to me. And then just as I was getting it back together inside, he whispered, "But I love ya." As he let go of me he said out loud, "I hope ya hang in there, 'cause I think you're gonna make it."

That was the first time that anyone, in an honest way, had confronted me about all of the bullshit I was throwing around. It was also the first time anyone had given me the simple truth about myself. This guy saw right through my pretenses. He saw through the chameleon-like protective coloration I had put on, and he saw behind the facade I wore to keep everyone at a distance. It felt like someone had just whacked me up one side of my head with a baseball bat while hitting me on the other side with a powder puff.

Suddenly, I heard a little voice inside me say, "This guy really cares about me." It was my little kid talking, my uncritical spontaneous God-given intuitive self. Surprisingly enough, I didn't recoil from the experience. I didn't back away or try to rationalize. I didn't even try to discount the event by being critical of the big-bellied truck driver ("brain-damaged, no doubt"). Flashing a lame, insincere smile and saying, "Thanks" I got the hell out of that meeting.

"This guy really cares about me."

And then the next thought that crossed my mind was, *"I wish my father would hug me."* This wish had always been there, a dormant yearning. But now, for the first time, I was willing to acknowledge it — to myself. What's more, I thought, "I don't have to go through life just wishing this could happen. I could make it happen. I could give him a hug."

To some it may sound a bit strange. I mean, why would a 25-year-old therapist recovering from chemical dependency get all worked up over a simple thing like hugging his father?

I'll tell you why. Because I am a co-dependent, an adult child of an alcoholic. Because like so many in our culture, I grew up in a troubled home filled with the dysfunctional rules of co-dependency. That's why.

Moreover, because of my co-dependent family history, I now realize that much of my childhood had been lost. I learned young to take care of myself and to do without the important nurturing that children need to get from their parents.

Caught between a hug and a hard place.

Adult children of alcoholics are in a constant conflict over what they experience as a crazy separation within their own spirit. They grow up intellectually and many of them learn the social skills required in order to look healthy — but, like me, they're faking it most of the time and guessing at what's normal.

Beneath that surface and behind that veneer is a chameleon-like identity. For example, I could go to church and be one man and then go someplace else and be another, but as far as what's on the inside, a chameleon doesn't change.

Creating Chameleons:
The Role of a Troubled Family System

On the surface there's nothing particularly bizarre or strikingly unusual about the co-dependent adult child. There are at least 28 million adult children of alcoholics alone, who are functioning out there in positions of responsibility, positions of government, education, mental health, business and industry, and so on. In short, there are a lot of people who've suffered the experience of growing up in troubled families, in troubled family systems.

There are roughly four types of troubled family systems that seem to stand out as prime breeding grounds for co-dependency:

I. *Alcoholism and Chemical Dependency:*
In the beginning, the concept of co-dependency grew out of observing the coping behaviors of individuals and families touched by alcoholism. Usually the label of "co-dependent" was given to a spouse or child of an alcoholic. In recent years, however, we have come to see co-dependency as a condition not solely linked to the alcoholic marriage or family system. Even so, it was out of the field of alcoholism and chemical dependency that our initial understanding of co-dependency first grew.

Today we recognize that the threads of co-dependency are subtly woven into the social fabric of our culture. To the degree that co-dependency does pervade our social order, we have begun to recognize its nature as one that stands independent of any single issue such as alcoholism. If this were not so, how could we explain the on-going difficulties in living which many alcoholics experience long after they have stopped drinking?

Could it be that "dry drunk" and co-dependency are one and the same?

Or on another level, how could we explain the emergence of co-dependent patterns in families who have never known alcoholism?

In simple terms, it is apparent that the alcoholic and/or chemically dependent family is only one system in which co-dependency thrives.

II. *The Emotionally or Psychologically Disturbed Family System:*

Whether the craziness of a family member is real or imagined (psychosomatic), co-dependency is the product of having that person inside the family running around and acting out in inconsistent, unpredictable and crazy ways. These kinds of families affect the lives of children in much the same way as an alcoholic family does.

III. *The Physically Abusive, Sexually Abusive Family System:*

In these families co-dependency arises because personal boundaries are constantly being violated. A family member's personal respect and integrity are seriously compromised by the threat of some impending physical or sexual violence. Small wonder that children from these families do not develop fully as people and so enter adulthood ill-prepared to handle many of the responsibilities which our society demands of all adults.

IV. *The Fundamentalistic or Rigid Dogmatic Family:*

These overly controlled family systems tend to operate on a narrow track. They are rigidly constructed and offer their members only a one-dimensional view of the world — a view that stresses order, discipline, regimentation, and, above all, sameness. The result is that the children in these families grow up to be little sergeants

---

If we see these threads of co-dependency woven into the underlying fabric of our culture, we can begin to understand why so many in our culture grow up and become alcoholics, overeaters, workaholics, sexual addicts or relationship-addicted.

---

or little clones. It's what Erickson calls "forclosed identity" or what I call a frozen identity state.

I'd guess that 80 percent of these folks are probably engaged in these addictive and compulsive patterns as a kind of medication for the unresolved psychological and emotional pain of their past. Daily they seek relief from the dissonance, pain and anxiety they experience every day over these bits of unfinished personal history.

The separation between how we *feel* at one level and what we *believe* at another is the source of our anxiety. It's the gulf between what we believe we ought to do and should be doing, and what we believe others would say is the right thing for us to do. It's the difference between a forced choice and a free choice. Between pretense and honesty.

The co-dependent is constantly pretending that things are fine when things are falling apart.

I have no doubt that there are real genetic factors behind alcoholism and other forms of chemical dependency. But I don't believe that even someone who was born with all that genetic loading and as a result becomes an alcoholic, would have to practice their alcoholism or addiction long before they would also have to find or create a new co-dependent system to support their alcoholism. Predictably, this new system would operate on the same kind of rules that any long-standing co-dependent family would operate on.

Ultimately, one way or another — whether the alcoholism came first or second — the system which supports such an illness will be co-dependent through and through. In a sense, the parents and the rules they live by must be seen as *Architects of a Co-dependent System.* If we study closely the four co-dependent family systems previously mentioned, we can begin to see some common patterns, similar designs of form and function, in the co-dependent family. We can trace the familiar blueprints of co-dependency and clearly examine the structure of the family rules that rule.

PART TWO

Major Features
of Co-dependency

Chapter 2

Co-dependency: What Is It?

Co-dependency is a term that has been widely used within the chemical dependency field over the past several years. Originally, "co-dependency" was used to describe the person or persons whose lives were affected as a result of their being involved with someone who was alcoholic or chemically dependent. The "co-dependent" spouse or child or lover of someone who was chemically dependent was seen as having developed a dysfunctional pattern of coping with life, a constricted and often self-destructive pattern inexorably linked to someone else's drug or alcohol abuse. The now familiar co-dependent strategies of minimizing, projection, intellectualizing or totally denying problems were seen as classic coping reactions to the chemically dependent person's maladaptive behavior.

But now many professionals are coming to understand that co-dependency can emerge from *any* family system where certain overt (spoken) and covert (unspoken) rules exist — rules that interfere with the normal process of emotional, psychological, behavioral and spiritual development. Rules that close off and discourage healthy communication, rules that eventually destroy a person's ability to form a trusting relationship within themselves or between others.

Co-dependency is a pattern of living, coping and problem-solving created and maintained by a set of dysfunctional rules within the family or social system. These rules inter-fere with healthy growth and make constructive change very difficult, if not impossible.

Common Problems for Co-dependents

The following is a list of some common problems for co-dependents. It is not an exhaustive or comprehensive list of problems, but most co-dependents will readily recognize and resonate to the patterns:

1. Difficulty in accurately identifying feelings: "Am I angry or sad or hurt or what?" "Am I truly depressed, or disappointed, or appropriately sad?" "Am I really frightened, or is my fear just an act?"

2. Difficulty in expressing feelings: "I feel angry, but it isn't safe to let other people know." "Anger is not okay." "I feel depressed, really down, but I can't talk with anyone — they wouldn't understand . . . They might think that I was weak."

3. Difficulty in forming or maintaining close or intimate relationships: "I want to be close to others but I'm afraid of being hurt or rejected." "I'm not bright enough (good-looking enough, rich enough) to run with that crowd."

4. Perfectionism — unrealistic expectations for self and others: "I never do anything right, I just screw up everything I do." "If I can't paint a perfect picture (write a poem, dance perfectly, and so on), then I just won't do it at all." "If he/she really loved me, they would have done it better."

5. Rigidity in behavior and/or attitudes: "I'm too old to change." "Even though I'm not happy with my life, I don't know any other way, so why change." "There's only one right way to do things (like being a man, being a woman, raising a child, having sex, or getting to heaven), and that's my way." "It was good enough for my parents and it's good enough for me."

6. Difficulty in adjusting to change. "I'll never forgive him for making me move away from our old house."

"He's not really going to stay sober, so I'm not going to open myself up again." "I don't know why things have to keep changing anyway."

7. Feeling overly responsible for other people's behavior and feelings: "It's my fault Sue killed herself. If only I had . . ." "I can't leave her — she'll never be able to handle it." "I should apologize to my friends for what Frank said to them yesterday."

8. Constant need for other's approval in order to feel good about self: "Just tell me what you want from me and I'll do it if it will make you happy." "I'll never be able to show my face around here again if I don't get accepted to the university." "Maybe if I become a doctor like my Dad he'll be proud of me."

9. Difficulty making decisions: "I can't decide, I don't want to make mistakes." "When I have to make hard choices, my mind just freezes up and my brain feels numb and paralyzed."

10. Feeling powerless, as if nothing I do makes any difference: "It's a no win situation. No matter what I do, I lose." "What's the point in putting myself out, no one will remember."

11. A basic sense of shame and low self-esteem: "When I make a mistake, it's just another example of what a worthless person I really am." "I come from a screwed up family, so there must be something wrong with *me*."

12. Avoidance of conflict: "If I tell him how I feel, he might leave me." "I have to act as if I agree, or they will get angry at me."

Paradoxical Co-dependency

Because many co-dependent people appear to be so self-sufficient, strong, and in control of their lives, a colleague of mine, John Friel, has called this pattern "paradoxical dependency." The paradox: Beneath the public image of strength and security often lies the opposite feeling of insecurity, self-doubt, and confusion.

"Everyone thinks I'm so strong, and all of my friends and relatives come to me with their problems," say many co-dependents. Then they add, "But if my friends and relatives only knew the real me, they would be very disappointed. Sometimes it's all I can do just to get through each day."

Another common worry: "I just know something's going to go wrong." Outwardly competent and together, inwardly they feel dread and foreboding. Co-dependents tell me they feel like they're not going to live until they're 18. Or 21. Or 32.

Insecurity manifests itself in other ways — in dreams, for example. Co-dependents tell me about dreams, repetitive dreams, of showing up half-dressed in class. Or they dream that they've registered for the class and it's the end of the term and there's a test — and they never went to a single class meeting, never cracked a book, never saw a lecture note. Or they dream they're running down a never-ending alleyway, they're being chased — by something repulsive and hideous.

All of which metaphorically suggests very clearly that what the person's having in subconscious awareness is that they are arriving fragmented in the world, not arriving as a whole person. And they are being chased down inside by a part of them that waits to be embraced as accepted and loved. A child-like part that longs to be recognized but is afraid to be seen.

To be more specific, here are several examples of dreams told to me by Denise, one of my co-dependent clients.

Dream One:

I am with a group of people, including my husband and our boys. We are loading onto buses to go somewhere to perform in a parade. I am run over by a bus, and I am lying paralyzed in the road. Someone picks me up and lays me on the floor of one of the buses. At that point, I realize that I've been cut in two, but only half of me seems injured. Ignoring what had just taken place, we drive on to the parade and everyone (including my husband, the boys and the uninjured half of me) gets off the bus and we all go on

*to the parade — leaving the injured, paralyzed part of me behind
on the floor of the bus . . . uncared for. I get a half block away and
I am filled with sorrow, because I have abandoned the injured me. I
know that this is wrong and not what I want to do. I realize that
the injured me is grievously hurt and is much more important than
the parade. I turn back, leaving the people I am with, and return to
care for the injured me. I get a doctor to give medical treatment and
I stay with the injured me, stroking her head, holding her hand,
and giving her comfort.*

Reflecting on her dream, Denise explained, "This dream
is very meaningful to me. Other people have left me, but I
don't focus on that fact. *I have abandoned myself.* I realize
that, and how serious my wounds are, and I choose to go
back. I nurture and comfort the child within me. I love her
and take care of her. The dream fills me with peace."

Denise's second dream depicts her determination to stay
healthy:

Dream Two:

*I am walking down a road, going downhill in a forest. It is
absolutely pitch-dark, and I can see nothing. I am not alone, I
have my inner child with me. I feel peaceful, unafraid. As we
proceed, we are attacked by a pack of fierce dogs — leaping,
snapping, snarling at us. I hold my child close, turning her
around to face me — away from the dogs — and I cross my arms
protectively over my inner child, we continue walking, and again
I am unafraid.*

How does this happen? Why is our perception of our real
self so different from the image we show other people? How
did we learn to live this way?

The co-dependent learns to do only those things that will
garner the approval and acceptance of other people. It is as
if some internal command system takes over and directs the
co-dependent according to a script that says:

"If I act like a good person, if I go to school, if I dress
right, if I act according to the rules of social edicts, then

somehow, some way, some day, I will receive something for all my efforts."

The need for love, acceptance, approval and recognition becomes the transcendent values.

Unfortunately, following this script has a cost. In this process of relentless approval-seeking, we gradually deny much of who and what we really are. Always alert and focused on others to get our needs met, we never have time to focus on ourselves in any other than a superficial way. And this has obvious consequences for how we see ourselves, how we view others and how we get along in the world.

Chapter 3

Learning to be Co-dependent

When I say that co-dependency originates in the family system, I mean that some — or all — of the characteristics listed previously are transmitted to family members through a set of dysfunctional rules. We learn these rules just as we learn how to ride a bike or drive a car or roller skate. We learn the rules through daily repetition and practice as we are growing up.

Let's take a look at perfectionism and the rule that says "We must do everything perfectly." Now, it's okay to expect most things to be done correctly most of the time. But many people make themselves very unhappy by expecting everything to be done perfectly every time. They expect every minor detail to go exactly as they had planned.

We learn the perfectionistic habits of co-dependency from our family. If Dad yells and screams about every little task or job he gives us to do and always yells at us about the way we do it, then in time we may come to think that even perfect isn't good enough. Or if Mom and Dad do everything according to a rigid unyielding schedule, then we may also begin to regiment everything in our lives.

After a while we can't feel relaxed or comfortable unless the picture is hung perfectly straight or the house is perfectly clean. Every detail becomes a major issue. Eventually, we begin to believe that every mistake we make is a personal reflection of who we are or what we're worth. In time we may start saying to ourselves over and over, "If only I were prettier or smarter or more athletic . . . if only I was more . . . then everything would be okay." It's virtually impossible for us to feel good about ourselves if we are always judging who we are by somebody else's standards of perfection. Especially if those standards seem forever out of reach.

Whether we call it approval-seeking, people-pleasing, or simply ass-kissing — this kind of behavior is a big problem for all too many of us co-dependent types. This kind of "flaming co-dependent" behavior, as I call it, reflects a deeply-seated, private and often unconscious belief that the road to love, belonging, acceptance and success is dependent on our ability to do what we *think* others want or expect us to do.

The practicing co-dependent looks at "doing for others" as a means to achieve these goals. Unfortunately, those we "do for" and those who we are trying to please are often not as concerned about our welfare as they are about their own.

The proverbial carrot of success is a cunning, baffling and powerful force in the co-dependent's life. For the co-dependent who believes that okayness depends on his or her ability to meet the real or imagined needs of others, this approval-seeking or people-pleasing behavior becomes a mood-altering drug of choice.

Once addicted, the co-dependent becomes blind to the reality of his behavior and to the things that really count, eg., self-respect, self-esteem, self-worth and self-love. Operating under a sincere delusion that people-pleasing will bring them what they want, co-dependents become willing participants in a losing game. Instead of success or joy, the co-dependent approval-seeker inevitably ends up angry, hurt, misunderstood, rejected, used, abused, and abandoned.

Take, for example, the classic story of Edith, an honest, dedicated, loyal and committed employee, wife and mother, who for 20 years dutifully fulfilled her every responsibility. No sacrifice was too great for her. To what end?

Edith lost her job, replaced by a computer. Her marriage fell apart when her husband found another woman. Edith sacrificed everything for her children, but they have grown up to be independent, free spirits who have no use for her advice and little time for her companionship.

She did everything right, just like Mom and Dad had told her, and look what she got for all her trouble. Edith gave it all, never thinking of herself, doing everything for her boss, her spouse, and her children.

"It's not supposed to turn out this way," Edith thinks, her heart full of bitterness and recriminations. "It isn't fair. Why did they do this to me? Where did I fail? What did I do wrong?"

Perhaps the only honest answer is that Edith, like other co-dependent approval-seekers, forgot to be there for herself over those 20 people-pleasing years. She did the best she could according to the rules. Too bad her parents had not given her a more realistic view of what it means to be true to yourself.

As far as her job is concerned, there had been times when she had seen the handwriting on the wall — change was in the air, but ostrich-like she stuck her head in her papers, praying that her loyalty and dedication would count for something. And there had been many times when she sensed that things were not going well in her marriage and family. But she didn't admit it. Edith was too eager to please, too determined to keep up appearances, too set in her ways to rock the boat.

Her mistake? She didn't listen to herself, she believed that taking care of others and doing what she had been told to do would guarantee stability and bring her happiness.

The people-pleasing co-dependent character in this story was not just a victim. In many ways Edith had become a *volunteer*. She had stuck it out through *"thin and thin,"* just as she had seen her parents do. Edith's worst crime was that in the process she had abandoned herself.

The life she lived was not her own.

To drive home a point, consider the case of a man I'll call

Jeremy. Jeremy grew up never learning from his father that he was okay, never getting a glimmer of approval, never getting any recognition that he measured up. For as long as Jeremy could remember, he had been trying to get his father's approval. In high school, Jeremy played football because his father had played. Jeremy despised the game, but he never quit, believing all through school that one day his father would be proud of him.

In college, Jeremy studied history. He graduated at the top of his class and like his father, Jeremy went on to law school to become a trial attorney. Even though Jeremy hated being a lawyer, he hoped that his accomplishments would finally earn his father's respect.

Soon after passing the bar exam, Jeremy married the girl next door, the girl his father had always hoped Jeremy would marry. Jeremy didn't really love her, but, as usual, the little boy in Jeremy was trying to get his father's approval.

Jeremy had ten unhappy years of marriage, two children — grandchildren for his father — and a mediocre career as a lawyer. Then his father died. Jeremy never succeeded in pleasing the old man, and without his father's love to strive for, his life went into a tailspin.

Jeremy felt he had failed. He was filled with regret. "If only I had been smarter," he thought. "If only I had been more athletic, if only I had been a more aggressive lawyer. then . . ."

Then what? . . . "Then he would have appreciated what I've done. Then he would see that I did it all for him. *Then he would have loved me!*"

Jeremy had done everything his father wanted, but it was never enough. Or was it?

This unfortunate script, like the story of Edith, is a clear example of living your life according to what you believe someone else wants. It's the ultimate co-dependent set-up to fail.

After all was said and done, after all the blaming was over, and after all the years of soul-searching and therapy,

Edith and Jeremy came face to face with themselves. The bottom line: They both had abandoned themselves. Like dependent children they did what they had been taught to do, automatically, almost by rote. Believing in the lie of this approval-seeking script, they were caught in a self-destructive co-dependent current.

Children are not co-dependent, they're just needy and dependent. For little children, approval-seeking is a normal behavior. As children, we lack the ability to be independent. But as emancipated individuals, we have a choice and so to choose the co-dependent path is to choose freely. Only adults, then, can truly be co-dependent. They have a choice. Children are the victims in a troubled family, adults are volunteers.

To borrow a quote from the recent movie WAR GAMES, "The only way to win the Game is not to play." How we treat ourselves and others is a direct result of the rules we learned as we were growing up. How we handle stress and conflict as adults is the result of how we learned to handle stress and conflict as kids. *But how we choose to handle them in the present is up to us.*

CO-DEPENDENCY:

The denial or repression of the real self based on an erroneous assumption that love, acceptance, security, success, closeness, and salvation are all dependent upon one's ability to do "the right thing."

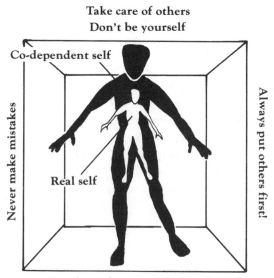

"The co-dependent is a spirit divided from itself."

The three dimensional box surrounding the figure represents the restrictive rules that imprison the co-dependent and prevent him or her from being real.

PART THREE

Co-dependency and Family Rules

Chapter 4

Stuck in Co-dependency

Let's examine some of these rules that keep us stuck in co-dependency.

1. It's not okay to talk about problems.
2. It's not okay to talk about or express our feelings openly.
3. Communication is best if indirect, with something or someone acting as messenger between two other people. This is called *triangulation*. It's you and me and the kids; you and me and the job; you and me and the checkbook; never just you and me.
4. Unrealistic expectations — Always be strong, always be good, always be perfect, always be happy.
5. Don't be selfish.
6. Do as I say, not as I do.
7. It's not okay to play or be playful.
8. Don't rock the boat.
9. Don't talk about sex.

These rules all serve to protect and isolate us from other people.

They prevent us from sharing and exploring our real thoughts and feelings and they keep us from getting close to others. People who grow up according to these rules have a difficult time believing that there are actually some families where it is all right to be yourself, talk freely about problems or express feelings openly, or make mistakes without harsh, sarcastic criticism or punishment. They don't realize that there are families where it is both routine and okay to be vulnerable and to ask for help.

Rules are a necessary part of maintaining order in life, and in this respect, we could not live without them. For example, there could be no creativity without discipline. There could be no freedom without limits. I do not question the *need* for rules in a family, but I want to raise questions about how those family rules are used and misused. And I want to draw attention to the consequences of the crazy-making family rules we live by.

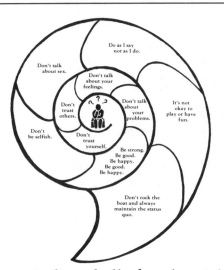

Within the spiraling shell of co-dependent rules there is an unclear identity, an underdeveloped sense of self, that waits for an opportunity to evolve and grow. Before this suspended, questioning self can begin to move towards clarity and resolution it must be emancipated from the controlling influence of any dysfunctional co-dependent rules that bind it.

Chapter 5

A Closer Look at
The Rules of Co-dependency

Rule 1:

**It's not okay to
talk about problems.**

We learn the no-talk rule in two ways. First, our parents may come right out and say, "What happens in this house is no one else's business, so keep your mouth shut."

More commonly, we learn this rule by watching our parents. Mom and Dad don't talk about problems, although tension may be hanging heavy in the air. We intuitively feel the tension, we experience the walking-on-eggshells feeling, but no one ever directly confronts the real cause of our problems. We end up fighting over small things that have little or nothing to do with the reality of our situation. It's not long before we learn that certain things are just better left unsaid.

Sometimes when a difficult subject comes up, we just disappear, get quiet, bury ourselves in television or try to change the topic.

The don't-talk rule in my family was more than just a subtle reality, it was like sharing our home with a hippopotamus. Whenever two or more of us were together, the hippo was there, too. So we practiced silence, aimed at keeping our unwelcome houseguest happy.

As a family, we had learned from past experience that to talk about the hippo — in this case, my mother's alcoholism — was to invite trouble. The truth of the matter was that to talk about one hippo was to inadvertently invite even more hippos into the house. Hippos like divorce, physical violence, rejection, or possibly even death. Consequently, the mere mention of alcoholism was to risk a full-scale stampede of rowdy hippopotami. Instead of just one hippo in the living room, we'd end up with a herd of hippos galumphing throughout the house. No one in my family wanted to take that chance.

For ten years we tiptoed around the hippo of alcoholism that was a living presence in our house. And we took every precaution to avert a stampede. Needless to say, life with a hippo made us anxious, wary, and distrustful. We always walked on thin ice, careful not to mention the hippo sitting there. Life with a hippo took its toll on all of us.

Sound familiar? Well such is the life of a person or family that operates on the "Don't Talk" rule.

The no-talk rule eventually causes us to avoid our problems or deny that we have any problems. It fosters a feeling of impending doom, typified by knots in the stomach, free-floating anxiety, headaches and sleeplessness.

We become emotionally numbed. Since we're not supposed to talk about our problems, we don't. We think that if we do admit to having a problem, then we are also admitting that something is horribly wrong with us that is not wrong with other people. If we admit to having a problem, then we open ourselves up to be judged by others as being weak or unhealthy. Ultimately, this denial or our basic situation fosters a deep sense of personal shame. Shame about things which otherwise should be viewed as very normal responses to living in a troubled family. We lose our perspective — namely, that people, *all people*, have problems.

The most frustrating and saddening aspect of the "no-talk" rule is the fact that we learn to avoid our problems. Obviously, we can't do much about our problems unless we can first acknowledge that they exist. If we can't talk about what's going on, then we will just have to go on denying and avoiding. The truth about life is that things are either getting better or they are getting worse. When you can't talk about the things that bother you, then you are likely to act them out. And the typical consequence of acting them out is that things get worse.

Don't let anyone see

Keep it inside

Rule 2:

It's not okay to talk about or express our feelings openly.

Historically, emotional expressiveness has not been a highly valued trait in American society. For men, a strong, silent image is admired. And while women are given more latitude in expressing their emotions, girls are taught at a young age that certain emotions, such as anger, are not ladylike and not acceptable.

So when it comes to expressing our true feelings, Americans of all ages — both men and women — are somewhat restrained as a result of certain cultural expectations.

In families with unresolved chemical dependency and co-dependency issues, this emotional blocking is an even greater problem. Expressing feelings is hard enough, but especially so when the spoken or unspoken rules make it clear that we just "don't." Instead we learn to stuff it. Our feelings get buried and our emotional lives become like a mine field that's all fenced in, with "No Trespassing" and warning signs posted everywhere.

We don't go into feelings, we don't explore them, and we don't talk about them. We learn to block our emotions when we hear statements like, "Big boys don't cry," or "Keep that up and I'll really give you something to cry about."

But we also receive this message in more subtle ways. When a frightened child tries to crawl into his father's lap, Dad gets tense. He feels uncomfortable with his own feelings and as a result finds it difficult to deal with his child's fear. His back arches and his shoulders stiffen. He is unreceptive. While Dad may not have said anything overtly, he may end up conveying his discomfort to his child. Dad can handle closeness as long as it's at arm's length.

In turn, the child becomes remote and unexpressive. The youngster needs his father's attention and nurturing, but the subtle non-verbal language of his parent tells the child that his needs are not okay. Why continue to be rejected? Why continue to be hurt? Who needs this kind of pain in his life? These are the questions the child's behavior conveys. In time the lesson learned by the child is: "Don't show your feelings around Dad."

If left unchallenged, this rule can and often does generalize to the global caution: "Don't show feelings around anyone." Danger lurks everywhere.

What is the result of denying and stifling our feelings? For one thing, we may come to believe that it is better for us to deny what we feel rather than to risk letting someone else see who we really are inside.

Eventually this cutting off of our emotional selves becomes so complete that even *we* no longer know who we really are. Our heads tell us one thing — like we don't care what others think of us — while our bodies unconsciously begin to tell us something else. We develop things like tension headaches, ulcers, high blood pressure, rashes, sleep problems, back pain or free-floating anxiety. We lose all our spontaneity and become so cut off from our true feelings, that we can't really see how they are affecting us.

I've heard it said that the opposite of spontaneity is depression. If this is true, then there must be one hell of a lot of depressed adult children co-dependents walking around out there. Worse yet, most of them probably don't even know it. Who are these amiable-looking sleep-walkers? I call them *the smiling depressed.*

Rule 3:

Don't address issues or relationships directly.

Co-dependents learn to communicate indirectly, with one person acting as messenger between two others (triangulation).

Sometimes this kind of triangulation also develops around everyday issues, so that we end up talking about "you and me and the kids," "you and me and the job," or "you and me and the checkbook."

What's so wrong with this scenario? Doesn't it include the children in the emotional lives of the parents?

Yes, it does. But not in a healthy way. Ideally, parents should be able to talk directly to one another without having to draw the children or some other third party into the middle of their conflicts.

Children in reality have very little power over their parents, yet the child who must live within the dysfunctional reality described above is a child destined to be burdened with the responsibility of trying to "fix things up" between his non-communicating parents. He gets caught in the middle. If he doesn't get Dad's message across to Mom, he feels that he has let Dad down. And if Mom reacts negatively, he winds up on the receiving end of all the anger and rejection she really wants to direct toward Dad. Either way, both parents are using the child to avoid having to face each other.

If practiced on a regular basis, this type of indirect co-dependent communication pattern will produce both confusion and guilt for all concerned. Messages and feelings get mixed up, and the innocent child, trapped in a no-win situation, ends up feeling somehow responsible for the lack of communication between the two parents.

When the situation finally explodes, as eventually it always does, the children are left thinking they are the cause of their parents' troubles. For the child these mistaken thoughts become the seeds of guilt that eventually germinate and grow into shame.

Rule 4:

Always be strong, always be good, always be perfect.

Above all, this rule embodies unrealistic expectations. Success and achievement are important to most of us. We want things to go right. And most of us have a fairly good idea of how we think things should be done. Sometimes, though, we begin to believe that there is only one right way to do things. What's worse is that we begin to believe that even perfect isn't good enough.

What happens in some families is that we create an ideal in our heads about what is good and right and best, but this ideal is so far removed from what is possible and realistic that we wind up punishing ourselves and others because our expectations are not met.

We begin to nag and criticize and push and analyze and cajole. We become deeply disappointed. We even begin to blame ourselves for not being able to get other people to do the things we want so that our expectations will be met. In time, everyone is unhappy with us. Live and let live is perhaps the most difficult principle for us to practice as co-dependents, because we want and need to control everything.

For the co-dependent, the locus of control, that is to say, the sense of being in control, is external, focused outside the self. In other words, the co-dependent has a sense that the real control over his life comes from external sources, not from inner resources. Thus the co-dependent spends a great deal of time trying to control what is often uncontrollable. Little things, you know . . . like other people.

In the co-dependent reality, being okay and feeling together inside requires that we maintain control over things on the outside. Letting go is a frightening thing for the co-dependent who sincerely believes that without his or her ability to control and manage the outside world, all needs, unconscious and unnecessary as many of them are, would not be met.

Take, for example, the individual who has believed all his life that being loved by others depends on what you can do for them. This means, of course, that if I no longer do the things which I believe are a prerequisite to receiving love, then it follows that I will no longer be loved.

This is the psychology of conditional love, and for the co-dependent it's a major obstacle to overcome on the road to recovery.

In simple terms, it could be said that the co-dependent endeavors to do the right or expected thing in order to get the love they so desperately need. Long range recovery, to a large degree, depends on the reversal of this co-dependent psychology of conditional love. Ideally, it should be that you and I seek out the right or proper direction in life because we feel loved in the first place.

Rule 5:

Don't
be selfish.

For the co-dependent who grows up in a family system where this rule is rigidly applied to every situation, feelings of guilt and shame are certain to emerge.

We learn to view ourselves as wrong for placing our needs before the needs of others.

It is very hard for co-dependents to accept the idea that it's okay to think of our own needs first. Normally, there are times in life when it makes good sense to take care of ourselves first. This is true in the case of a co-dependent partner of an alcoholic who goes into counseling knowing that to be selfish and seek help for themselves is to risk being rejected by their spouse.

If we believe our own needs are wrong, then we will never be able to ask directly for those needs to be met. Consequently, the co-dependent often tries to get personal needs met through manipulating or by taking care of others. Eventually this makes us overly dependent on others and our whole existence becomes wrapped up in caretaking. Without somebody to take care of, we feel we have no purpose or worth. The more time we spend taking care of others, the less time we have to devote to our own needs. We get lost in the shuffle, and in the end we don't even know that we have needs — much less know what these needs might be.

Ultimately, if those we are serving fail to recognize and

appreciate our sacrifices on their behalf, we may start to feel resentful, abused and taken for granted. This in turn leaves us feeling even more guilty and ashamed for being angry. With no apparent way out of this vicious co-dependent cycle, we try even harder to make up for all our inappropriate anger by doing more caretaking.

Because we feel so wrong inside for putting ourselves first, we continue to set ourselves up to be used. In the end, we feel resentful, bitter and angry. And still our needs go unmet.

Consider for a moment Miriam, a woman who grew up with the neglect, abandonment and abuse of an alcoholic father and whose mother never took a stand, but meekly tolerated the situation. As an adult child, Miriam thinks of her mom as a saint who will certainly get her reward in heaven and Miriam considers her father a sinner who will get his dues in some less glamorous place. Having learned well from her parents, Miriam chose to marry a man who will allow her to become the long-suffering saint just like her mother was. Based on what Miriam had experienced as a child, the role of martyr was a familiar and safe part to play. Her mother was the most selfless person Miriam had ever known. How could Miriam possibly do less? What a noble aspiration! Besides, to strive for less would be to let her sainted mother down. The fulfillment of this seemingly selfless script became Miriam's lifelong goal.

How do we escape from the merry-go-round of perpetual caretaking? To break the painful hold of the "don't be selfish" rule, we must first be "selfish" in a healthy way, by deciding to take care of ourselves.This means that in order to get free, we must stop trying to build up our own self-worth through the caretaking of others. We must stop neglecting our own needs. This may be difficult at first, because our self-esteem is dependent on taking care of others. But while the risk of change is great, the rewards are even greater. Loving your neighbor as yourself means that in order to truly love our neighbor we must first love ourselves.

Rule 6:

**Do as I say . . .
not as I do.**

This rule, more than any other, teaches us not to trust. If, as children, we are told by our parents to be honest, and then we see them being dishonest, we become confused and suspicious. We stop trusting and begin to count only on ourselves. We do this out of a need to protect ourselves from the emotional pain that results from our parents' inconsistency. What we come to know is that the only thing for sure is that nothing is for sure. "Don't let me catch you with drugs," we hear our parents threaten as they brandish a cigarette in one hand and a drink in the other.

"You kids behave yourselves," parents shout, then acting just like two little children themselves, they proceed to turn on each other with unrestrained fury.

"Wipe that sullen look off your face, young man," Mom snarls after moping around the house for two days with the same kind of look on her face. If Mom's look could kill, there would be no one left alive in the house.

In *The Road Less Traveled*, M. Scott Peck writes that the rule "Do as I say, not as I do," is one of the most destructive messages parents can give to their children: "If a child sees his parents day in and day out behaving with self-discipline, restraint, dignity and a capacity to order their own lives, then the child will come to feel in the deepest fibers of his being that this is the way to live. If a child sees his parents day in and day out living without self-restraint or self-discipline, then he will come in the deepest fibers of his being to believe that this is the way to live."

When our parents tell us lies and make promises to us they can't or won't keep, we begin to question our own worth. The child wonders, "Do they treat me that way because they don't love me?" If a child lacks trust in his parents' love, then it's not difficult to imagine how he might begin to feel insecure within himself and end up developing a real fear of abandonment in all his relationships.

As children, many of us who lived in the "Do as I say . . . not as I do" reality, ultimately came to believe that we were not worthy of our parents' love. Unable to count on our parents approval, and fearful of abandonment, we sought out new and indirect ways of getting our needs met. Conscious or otherwise, we began to manipulate others to give us validation and love. Believing that who we are inside is not good enough or deserving enough, we hide our unacceptable selves. We learn to do those things which we think will bring us approval from others. Once in place the private logic of "I am not okay" becomes the self-defeating foundation of our shame.

The most insidious and destructive part of this particular rule is how, by doing only what we think others want us to do, we end up abandoning ourselves. Inevitably we become divided inside and feel compelled to deny who we really are to others. Being a phony means that we can never know for sure if those people close to us really care about us. Or just the person that we pretend to be.

We live in constant fear of being rejected. "What if they should ever find out the truth?" The constant co-dependent efforts to do "right" at the cost of not being true to ourselves simply perpetuates and deepens our sense of shame. We co-dependents know a lot about the truth as a result of trying so hard to avoid it, but we find no relief from the emotional fallout or hangover of our lie because we never share the truth which divides us from ourselves.

We tell ourselves and others that it is important to be true to ourselves, but in reality we are not. We are thinly-disguised hypocrites. We do not do as we say.

Rule 7:

It's not okay to play.

From the very beginning, the co-dependent adult child believes that the world is a very serious place. Life is seen as difficult and almost always painful. Like all the co-dependent rules previously mentioned, this rule — "It's not okay to play" — lends itself well to the development of negative thinking and a view of ourselves as unlovable, boring, stupid, ugly, and wrong. Because of this, the co-dependent is always working twice as hard as everyone else just to feel okay. Having some project to work on or some crisis to deal with gives us a sense of purpose. In time, we become preoccupied with a smorgasbord of more or less urgent issues — our kids, our job, our friends, our health. And in time, we simply get lost in the shuffle.

Take, for example, one of the more classic co-dependent beliefs that what you do is somehow a measure of who you are. One's identity and sense of self-worth become inextricably linked to one's job. From this perspective, since play according to the co-dependent workaholic would be a stupid waste of time, then it follows that play would also be viewed as a threat to one's identity. Another phrasing of the rule might be: "Real (serious) people don't play."

When an adult co-dependent believes fervently in this philosophy, it becomes increasingly important to their feelings of okayness that they not be without something to do. It's okay to play if you are a child, but not if you are an adult. The longer we deny our need to play, the more we suffer. Ultimately, to play is to risk being spontaneous, and perhaps even foolish. For the co-dependent, letting their hair down is a frightening experience. Having fun is not *productive*, so having fun is *not okay*. Children growing up in troubled families are denied so much of their childhood that as a result of their need to care for themselves, they are in a hurry to grow up. Parents of these children often say about them that they are six years old going on 40. Being all grown up someday is important, but losing one's childlike ability to play is a difficult gift to recapture. After all, we tell ourselves, "Now you are an adult so you should act like one." The child in us wants to play, but we hold back, afraid that someone would think us foolish or childish. And so once again we abandon ourselves, but blame others for our inability to be spontaneous or genuine.

Rule 8:

Don't rock the boat.

Every family is a system. Each person in the family has a special part, like actors in a play. The family rules help each person to know his or her part. Family rules make it easier for us to know what is right, what is wrong, and at what age we should be doing certain things.

Stability is one of the positive results of healthy family rules. Balance. Equilibrium. The rules serve to keep everything in harmony, so when someone breaks a rule the entire family may become upset. Like the human body that feels

pain when it gets sick or hurt, the family system also experiences pain when the natural order of things is upset.

Natural order does not necessarily mean what is best or
most healthy. When Timmy gets a negative report from
school, or Mom gets a serious illness, the family rules say
that something should be done to restore the system to
some kind of balance. Mom and Dad talk to Timmy's
teacher; or Dad and the kids change their schedules to handle the work that Mom can't do. The system seeks balance.
All systems have this self-adjusting mechanism, this desire
for homeostasis. So the family adjusting to change is a
healthy quality.

In families where there are lots of unresolved issues such
as alcoholism, chemical dependency, physical or sexual
abuse, the system also seeks to maintain a type of balance,
but the balance it seeks to maintain is an unhealthy one.

The dysfunctional rules it fights so hard to hang onto
make it difficult for the people living in the system to face
their issues, to grow through their problems and to become
whole, healthy, autonomous human beings.

Take the case of Suzy, who becomes increasingly anxious
over her father's drinking and the fact that her parents are
fighting all the time. Unfortunately for Suzy, the rules of
her system say, "We don't talk about Dad's problems,"
and "We don't express our real feelings." So Suzy keeps
them inside.

Is Suzy doing something wrong, according to the family
system? No. Like the actor in a play, Suzy is doing her part
to keep the system in balance. She's not rocking the boat,
she's just trying to survive in a dysfunctional system.

In other words, the system seeks to maintain itself. The
flaw in this system is that the family rules do not allow for
healthy change. Dad doesn't want to give up drinking. Nobody wants to confront him about his drinking because it
might upset him, and besides, if Dad stopped drinking, then
everyone would have to change, and change — even change
for the better — is frightening. Yet with enough help and

support the fear of change can be overcome and recovery can take place.

"Don't rock the boat" is the all-encompassing rule, the master rule and gate-keeper who rides herd over all the other rules in the family. "Don't rock the boat," becomes the rule that rules. This simple but stern injunction, "Don't rock the boat!" locks each individual family member inside a set of unhealthy rules. If left unchallenged, these rules will inevitably suppress change, hinder growth, and obstruct any hope of recovery.

Chapter 6

Don't Talk About Sex

Sex! Now there's a subject that gets our attention. When you consider how little we express our true thoughts and feelings about this stimulating topic, it's not difficult to understand why it commands so much of our interest.

We have many rules and prohibitions regarding sex, but by and large the over-riding rule is "Don't talk about IT." And especially don't talk about Doing IT.

The social and cultural avoidance of this issue is a well-documented fact. Since the beginning, we have treated the whole subject of sex like a hot potato. Everyone's afraid of getting burned.

Did you know that just eleven weeks into the process of gestation, you and I are identifiable as male or female. Even before birth, our sexuality starts to play a significant role in our lives.

Despite this fact, and despite the fact that there is no single issue that will affect us more over the course of our lifetime than our sexuality, there is no issue that will get less attention.

For the co-dependent, the shame and anxiety associated with unresolved sexual issues is directly proportional to the length of time we have lived by the "don't talk" rules that surround us.

Our social and cultural history has long minimized the

importance of our sexuality and the basic need to talk about it.

In my family, this was certainly the case, and despite the alcoholism which pervaded our family system, I don't think we were all that different from the so-called "normal" family. My parents' values were very much a reflection on the cultural norms concerning sex. That is, sex was not a subject for polite conversation.

My sisters, my brother and I — all of us went through puberty without ever mentioning the obvious changes we were all going through. This was a very confusing time for me. It seemed like everything was different, but nothing outside had changed. At least nothing that anyone really wanted to talk about.

Sure indirectly, we all heard the less-than-subtle warnings about what might happen to us if we weren't careful. But we never got any clear or direct information about our emerging sexuality.

The question I would ask you and the question I sometimes ask audiences, "How many of you learned about sex from your parents? Now be honest . . . I mean really learned in detail about the real story." In the typical audience, almost no one raises their hand. Could you?

Then I ask, "How many of you learned from your friends, your brothers or sisters, from a book you found but shouldn't have had, or by mutual experimentation?" Still only a few hands go up.

At this point, it's clear that most of the people never raised their hands, so finally I ask, "How many of you still don't know?"

My own sex education began by reading some medical manuals that my father had brought home from his office and left around for us to find. He was a doctor, so I figure he thought that reading about IT from a manual was the best way to make sure that I learned where everything fit, so to speak.

Funny thing about that time of life — puberty, I mean —while you don't really know what it is you're looking for, you certainly seem to know what it is when you find it. I was no exception, and even though I couldn't understand half the words that I read in the manuals, the pictures I saw were worth a thousand words.

Naturally I couldn't keep such important stuff to myself, so I got on the phone and called my friends, Frank, Mark, Bruce and Steve. I had them meet me at the old tree fort, and there I gave them "Intro to Sex 101."

Steve was just a year or two younger than the rest of us and most of what I shared went right over his head. The part about sexual intercourse though really shook him up. I suppose the way I described it, it did sound kind of painful — the stabbing part and all.

More than a little frightened by the whole lesson, Steve ran home crying and told his parents. Bad news travels fast. When I got back home, my mother was all over my case. She took the forbidden book away, sent me to my room and told me never to talk about it again.

No, I didn't do as she had ordered, and like so many adolescents going through puberty, I took my sexuality and went underground. Gradually, I managed to put the facts of life together, no thanks to my parents, church or school. Experience was a good teacher, but the emotional and psychological tuition was high. In hindsight, a healthy model or understanding teacher could have certainly spared me a lot of pain. Obviously it was not okay for my parents to talk about sex.

Since our recoveries began, my parents and I have had many opportunities to talk about those years, and it is clear that the "No sex talk" rule had been a long-standing fixture in their lives. Not talking about sex was an old social rule and, for all our sakes, one that needed to be broken. After all, our sexuality — yours and mine — is a major part of understanding ourselves fully. If we can't talk about our sexuality, then we will likely be stifled in our search for a clear identity.

The attitudes, behaviors and beliefs of our primary caregivers — moms, dads, aunts, uncles or grandparents — play a significant role in the way that we perceive ourselves and the world around us. With regard to sex, it is apparent that these caregivers set the developmental stage for children. A clear and healthy understanding of sex and sexuality depends largely on our early experiences with these people.

I cherish the memories of my grandmother BeBe, bless her little heart. She was truly well-meaning, but she managed to create more confusion and shame for me than any other single person in my life.

One day while my sister Pam and I were preparing to take our weekly bath together — Pam was seven and I was six — my grandmother appeared suddenly out of nowhere and spoiled all our fun. We were chasing around trying to snap each other on the hind end with our towels, when just as we were about to enter the bathroom BeBe held out her arm and stopped me in my tracks.

Then she slammed the bathroom door behind my sister and said to me, "Young man, you should be ashamed of yourself. Your sister is a young woman and you should not be bathing with her."

The thought that we should not bathe together had never entered my mind, much less the thought that my seven-year-old sister was a young woman. Before I could respond, BeBe went on to say, "Besides, men do not take baths." I looked at her uncomprehendingly. "They take showers," BeBe said with great authority.

This must be true, I thought. After all I had never seen my dad in the tub. Only my mother. What did I know about the etiquette of bathing, the protocol of showers and baths? The idea that I could be a real man by using the shower sounded okay to me.

With this new thought in mind I gladly marched off to our other bathroom and prepared myself for the experience of a six-year-old's lifetime. As I closed the door of the shower behind me, I heard my grandmother say, "Now be quick about it and no fooling around."

Fooling around? The only thing I could think of was that being a man meant no more fun on bath-day. No matter, I was willing to pay the price. So I turned on the shower and began my passage into manhood. Then, through the torrents of water pouring over my head, I heard BeBe say, "And don't touch yourself!"

Take a shower, but don't touch yourself. Well, I was young, but not that young. I knew what she was talking about. Next I heard her say, "If you do — I'll know, because you'll grow black hair all over the back of your hands."

I looked at my hands and then at my private parts. How the hell do I wash myself if I don't touch myself? Becoming a man was quickly losing all its appeal. Worst of all was the fact that it hurt to pull all those black hairs off the backs of my hands. I was twenty-seven before I ever talked about that piece of history. Over the years I had touched myself a lot, but I never let a black hair grow on my hand.

I've worked with a lot of people in ten years as a therapist, and during that time I've heard all sorts of stories — many of them similar to the one I just shared. The rules about sex can be terribly destructive when they come to you in this way as a child.

Shame over our sexuality is largely due to our ignorance about it. What should be viewed as normal and healthy with respect to our sexuality is very often judged as bad and wrong simply because we are unable to talk about it. This shame will remain with us until we break out of the silence that surrounds the sexual dimensions of our real self.

READER/CUSTOMER CARE SURVEY

If you are enjoying this book, please help us serve you better and meet your changing needs by taking a few minutes to complete this survey. Please fold it and drop it in the mail.

As a special **"Thank You"** we'll send you news about new books and a valuable **Gift Certificate!**

PLEASE PRINT   C8C

NAME:_____

ADDRESS: _____

_____

TELEPHONE NUMBER: _____

FAX NUMBER: _____

E-MAIL: _____

WEBSITE: _____

(1) Gender: 1)_____Female 2)_____Male

(2) Age:
1)_____12 or under   5)_____30-39
2)_____13-15   6)_____40-49
3)_____16-19   7)_____50-59
4)_____20-29   8)_____60+

(3) Your Children's Age(s):
Check all that apply.
1)_____6 or Under   3)_____11-14
2)_____7-10   4)_____15-18

(7) Marital Status:
1)_____Married
2)_____Single
3)_____Divorced/Wid.

(8) Was this book
1)_____Purchased for yourself?
2)_____Received as a gift?

(9) How many books do you read a month?
1)_____1   3)_____3
2)_____2   4)_____4+

(10) How did you find out about this book?
Please check ONE.
1)_____Personal Recommendation
2)_____Store Display
3)_____TV/Radio Program
4)_____Bestseller List
5)_____Website
6)_____Advertisement/Article or Book Review
7)_____Catalog or mailing
8)_____Other_____

(11) What FIVE subject areas do you enjoy reading about most?
Rank: 1 (favorite) through 5 (least favorite)
A)_____ Self Development
B)_____ New Age/Alternative Healing
C)_____ Storytelling
D)_____ Spirituality/Inspiration
E)_____ Family and Relationships
F)_____ Health and Nutrition
G)_____ Recovery
H)_____ Business/Professional
I)_____ Entertainment
J)_____ Teen Issues
K)_____ Pets

(16) Where do you purchase most of your books?
Check the top TWO locations.
A)_____ General Bookstore
B)_____ Religious Bookstore
C)_____ Warehouse/Price Club
D)_____ Discount or Other Retail Store
E)_____ Website
F)_____ Book Club/Mail Order

(18) Did you enjoy the stories in this book?
1)_____Almost All
2)_____Few
3)_____Some

(19) What type of magazine do you SUBSCRIBE to?
Check up to FIVE subscription categories.
A)_____ General Inspiration
B)_____ Religious/Devotional
C)_____ Business/Professional
D)_____ World News/Current Events
E)_____ Entertainment
F)_____ Homemaking, Cooking, Crafts
G)_____ Women's Issues
H)_____ Other (please specify) _____

(24) Please indicate your income level
1)_____Student/Retired-fixed income
2)_____Under $25,000
3)_____$25,000-$50,000
4)_____$50,001-$75,000
5)_____$75,001-$100,000
6)_____Over $100,000

TAPE HERE DO NOT STAPLE

NO POSTAGE
NECESSARY
IF MAILED
IN THE
UNITED STATES

BUSINESS REPLY MAIL
FIRST-CLASS MAIL PERMIT NO 45 DEERFIELD BEACH, FL

POSTAGE WILL BE PAID BY ADDRESSEE

HEALTH COMMUNICATIONS, INC.
3201 SW 15TH STREET
DEERFIELD BEACH FL 33442-9875

FOLD HERE

((25) Do you attend seminars?
1)_____Yes   2)_____No

(26) If you answered yes, what type?
Check all that apply.
1)_____Business/Financial
2)_____Motivational
3)_____Religious/Spiritual
4)_____Job-related
5)_____Family/Relationship issues

(31) Are you:
1) A Parent?_____
2) A Grandparent?_____

Additional comments you would like to make:

_____
_____
_____
_____

N-CS   C8C

Chapter 7

Summing Up
The Family Rules

Water Seeks Its Own Level

The way we learn to live our lives and interact with others is acquired from our families as we grow up. The rules we have discussed are examples of some of the ways families can unconsciously create the atmosphere in which co-dependency or chemical dependency can develop.

Why do some people seem to escape the negative consequences? We don't know for sure, but it may be that they managed to form a secure attachment with someone outside the family system long enough to have gained the trust, support and courage necessary to choose healthier ways of living. Perhaps this other person was an aunt or an uncle, a grandparent or the parent of a friend.

The rules teach us how to live and solve problems. These rules are passed down from one generation to the next, not by heredity or genetics, but by learning . . . by watching and mimicking. Also the more we live with these rules, the more likely it is that we will begin to practice them in our own daily lives, and the more likely it is that we will find ourselves surrounded by other people who are caught up in the same kinds of rules.

Water seeks its own level, as they say, and so it is with co-dependency. Tragically, the more we experience living with these rules, the more we tend to internalize them and become separated from ourselves.

Family rules are the mechanism by which co-dependency is transmitted across the generations, and until the rules change, we will continue to see children who as adults lack a clear sense of self and who are destined to be co-dependent as a result.

Though it may seem a controversial thought to some, many professionals are beginning to realize that a large number of compulsive or agent-dependent individuals (ie, alcoholics, overeaters, workaholics, and so on) are beneath it all practicing co-dependents. More often than not, the compulsive or harmfully dependent person comes from a troubled family background where they learned the dysfunctional co-dependent patterns of survival that would later give rise to a dependency on work, food or alcohol.

Heredity aside, many of our young people today feel compelled to turn to mood-altering chemicals and other harmful compulsive behaviors in an effort to medicate the pain of living in a troubled family system.

In support of the notion that co-dependency is for many a pre-existing condition are the growing number of individuals who have begun the process of recovery from their primary dependency on food, alcohol, work or relationships, and have come to recognize that their next step is their recovery from co-dependency.

What many people call a "dry drunk" in the non-using chemically dependent person is, to me, no more than the on-going expression of their unresolved co-dependency. To the extent that the chemically dependent person may be reacting to the processes of withdrawal, we may consider his behavior and mood swings as part and parcel of a biochemical "dry drunk."

However, beyond the point of mere chemical withdrawal, we must recognize the dry drunk behavior as a language of co-dependency. This not-so-subtle shift in our thinking fits nicely with the old notion that abstinence or sobriety represent but a small fraction of our recovery. Perhaps no more than five percent of the recovery process and genuine sobriety can be attributed to the choice to stop drinking or to discontinue the misuse of mood-altering agents such as food, alcohol, sex or work. The remaining 95 percent of the process has to do with the individual's struggle to recover their emotional lives from the grip of co-dependency.

For this population, on-going relationship problems, irritability, immaturity and moodiness are all signs that the person is continuing to operate according to the dysfunctional co-dependent rules which say, "Don't talk," "Be perfect," "Don't rock the boat," and so on. For the child or the adult living under these dysfunctional rules, the normal process of identity development and maturity is stifled. In the most basic sense, *co-dependency is the product of delayed or interrupted identity brought about by the practice of dysfunctional rules.* Until we begin to live by a new and healthier set of family rules, the painful realities of living in a co-dependent lifestyle will continue.

PART FOUR
The Whole Fam-Damily

Chapter 8

The Whole Fam-Damily

The child who grows up in a troubled family, with all its dysfunctional rules — don't talk, don't rock the boat, and so on — is practically guaranteed to end up suffering from feelings of anger, hurt, loneliness, guilt and shame.

Fortunately, as children we learn to survive our troubled pasts by compensating for the many needs that were left unmet and the unconditional love not given. We learn to hide our feelings because we've gotten the message loud and clear that: "Real feelings are dangerous." And that: "It's not okay to be needy."

Growing up in a troubled family, we learn to live day by day with the constant fear of rejection, punishment abandonment or worse. It means we learn early on to live with the burden of free-floating anxiety that developed as a direct result of the on-going denial and repression of our true thoughts and feelings

---

Free-floating anxiety is
the symptom of a divided self.

Sincere Delusion and Survival Logic

We repeatedly — then habitually — choose to side-step the truth in order to avoid our pain and maintain the status quo. Ultimately, this choice forces us into a co-dependent state of sincere delusion.

As I pointed out earlier, sincere delusion is the worst kind of delusion precisely because it is sincere. We choose to lie, deny, procrastinate and avoid because we believe that the truth would be dangerous to our health. Survival, then, becomes our primary objective and we lose perspective. We sincerely believe that we must lie in order to survive. Tom, a recovering co-dependent adult child spoke about his delusion this way: "I see now that deceptiveness became a habit, second nature with me. I grew up feeling I had to be all things to all people, changing my self to fit what I thought were the demands of others. When I felt too much pressure, I withdrew, faded into the woodwork. I went through these contortions because I felt — honestly felt — that the truth would finish me off. Truth was the enemy. My co-dependent delusion and deception turned me into an invisible man, a divided spirit who would pass undetected through half his lifetime."

Unfortunately, we all know that there are lots of children like Tom, who did not make it through childhood unscarred or unscathed. Sadly enough, we also know that there are many more wounded spirits out there who will not make it in the future.

In this country we have some dangerous myths about children. One of the most prevalent and destructive is the myth that children are resilient. What tripe! I have a difficult time believing that children are not damaged by the dysfunctional behaviors of their parents. Things like abandonment, neglect, rejection or other forms of abuse leave lasting scars.

Animal studies have produced abundant evidence supporting the notion that physical touch, emotional comfort and other forms of parental nurturing are essential ingredients in the promotion of normal growth and development. These same ingredients are also essential for us humans.

Some researchers believe that we could actually predict

through observing the coping behaviors of young children who the children are that would be at high risk for the development of dysfunctional coping patterns later in life. No matter how we choose to look at it, it is clear that a child's early life experiences play a significant role in how they will function as adults.

Given the importance of early child development it is not difficult to see how the child who does not develop trust early on in life is likely to become the adult who does not trust. Without a basic trust in self or others, closeness, love, and intimacy are all but impossible.

Body By Bondo

How resilient are kids? Think of it this way: Get out of your chair, walk outside, take an 8-lb. sledgehammer and start beating on your car. Children from troubled families can be bruised and scarred in much the same way as your car would be bashed, scraped and battered by this exercise. The only difference would be that the emotional and psychological damage the child suffered might not show so clearly.

As a teenager back in the late 60s, a number of my friends and I were into fixing up old cars. To repair the body of these old clunkers we used a compound called Bondo, a plastic resinous mixture that was perfect for covering up all the dents and rust. If we applied the Bondo properly and sanded it down smoothly enough, we could then paint right over all the damaged areas and make the car look as though it were fresh off the showroom floor.

Unfortunately, after a year or so of hard driving and weather, the Bondo would begin to loosen, the paint would begin to crack, and ultimately the Bondo itself would separate and fall away. Our beautiful looking masterpiece was once again just an old wreck. Well, as they say, you can't judge a book by its cover — or a car by its paint job. In short, body by Bondo is to car as co-dependency is to people.

The way I see it, the co-dependent adult or co-dependent adult child is someone whose unresolved conflicts, like the damage hidden beneath the Bondo, will one day return to haunt them. Life can sometimes be a bumpy ride and a "co-dependent body by Bondo" just won't cut it over the long haul.

Fortunately, all human beings are resilient . . . to a point . . . but it would be a serious mistake to think that the human spirit, in particular the fragile spirit of a child, is resilient to the hideous abuses, tensions and emotional trauma of a troubled family.

In the literal sense resilient means returning to, or resuming, the original position or shape, capable of withstanding shock without permanent deformation or rupture.

If this is true, then children of a troubled family history are not truly resilient, but instead rather resourceful. Thank God, the child in us is such a creative, tenacious and persevering spirit. If you are one of those surviving co-dependent spirits, then I strongly suggest that you set aside some time — like right now, for example — and give the child inside you some credit and recognition for having helped you make it this far, credit for having done such a fantastic job of surviving. After all, it's only fair to give credit where credit is due, even if it has been a tad long in the coming.

The Resourceful Inner Child

One exercise I would recommend for starters is that you sit yourself down somewhere in front of a mirror and imagine that the reflection you see is your own inner child. Look straight into his or her eyes and say: "Thank you for not giving up."

Validating yourself in this way and beginning to develop a healthy relationship with your inner child is a crucial first step in the co-dependent's recovery process.

Do you recognize that your inner child really exists?

Some of us recovering folks have a difficult time visualizing the inner child as anything but evil or bad. We see the child as some ugly creature that needs to be exorcized or driven out of our lives. At best we see the inner child as a kind of superbrat, capable of doing great harm to anyone or anything that gets too close.

Still others in the adult child co-dependent population view the inner child as some kind of waif or wimp, huddled in some dark corner of the psyche, pathetic, powerless and forlorn.

I believe the inner child is a reservoir of strength, a repository of our best intuitions and an ultimate link to all that is divine and good in the world. Many are the stories I've heard about the ingenuity of children who have had to face the adversity and victimization of emotional, physical, sexual, and psychological abuse.

Necessity is the mother of invention and for the child growing up in a troubled family, the development of self-taught survival skills is an absolute necessity.

Children may be creative, tenacious, and persevering spirits, even survivors but they are *not* resilient in the truest sense. Wounds take time to heal.

The Chocolate Chip Cookie Solution

One of the more poignant stories I ever heard came from my sister Cindy, who, like me, had experienced many trials while growing up in our troubled family. One day Cindy began to tell me how she had always felt alone, particularly after coming home from school and walking into our big empty house.

I understood immediately what Cindy was saying, but it had never occurred to me that she had felt the same way. You see, our mother was no longer drinking, and so I had just assumed that things were better for Cindy than they had been for me. I had all but forgotten how much time we kids had spent alone, particularly during those early years of my mother's sobriety when she was struggling hard to get her own life back together. During that stage of my mother's recovery, both of our parents were away a lot. My mother had decided to go back to school, and my father was continuing to put long hours in at the office.

Looking back, I believe that these were important survival choices that they each felt they had to make. But for my sisters and me it meant being left alone a lot.

At any rate, as Cindy spoke, she went on to tell me how she had always wished that our family could be more like "Ozzie and Harriet" or "Leave It To Beaver." As different as some of our recollections are, Cindy and I both agreed that June and Ward Cleaver our parents weren't. Cindy had never been one to sit and suck her thumb, so whenever life didn't live up to Cindy's expectations, she would simply play make-believe. In the story she shared with me, her fantasy went like this: First of all, instead of coming home to an empty house, Cindy decided to pretend that while she was at school, Mom had been home baking her some chocolate chip cookies. To complete the fantasy, Cindy would hurry home from school, go directly into the kitchen, and bake a batch of those chocolate chip goodies. And then pretending to be Mom, Cindy would serve herself a big tray full of freshly baked cookies along with a glass of cold milk.

As a child, Cindy learned early that the only way to fill in the need-gaps — the only reliable way to get her needs met — was to take care of them herself, through fantasy if need be. Making believe was easier than living in her pain.

Like most recovering co-dependents, my sister has had to work hard to make peace with her past and put it to rest. To a large degree, her recovery has depended on her willingness to face the little girl in her history. The reunion between herself and the inner child of her alcoholic family history has, as it will for others, provided her with a way to re-parent herself and replace some of the missed moments.

Facing the Child Within

Facing the child of our troubled history is no easy task and more often than not I hear adult children say things like, "What's the sense of opening the door on the past" or

"It's too late to do anything now, I'm no longer a child."
When I hear these words, I know that the person speaking
has not yet faced the child within them. I also know that
until they do face this child, they will continue to live out a
self-defeating co-dependent lifestyle. You see, without a
healthy, accepting and loving relationship within yourself,
there is no room for self-actualization or a clear identity.
For the practicing co-dependent there is only a kind of
co-dependent pseudo-identity that is based on what you do,
who you know, how much you make, where you live, or
what religion you are. The co-dependent identity is an identity formed from the outside in, instead of from the inside
out. As a result the individual becomes dependent on the
outside realities in order to compensate for what is lacking
on the inside. Unfortunately . . .

If you are what you do, and then you don't, you aren't.

In the case of a co-dependent identity, it is not too difficult to understand why there is so much anxiety, fear, self-
doubt, paranoia, and insecurity about life. After all, if what
you are is dependent on what you do, then if you
don't . . . what's left?

For example, as a young man Jesse based his entire identity on his athletic ability. A superb athlete in high school,
he lettered in four different sports and he received a full
college scholarship to play basketball. He was a local hero,
and along with his hero status came certain perks . . . auto-
matic grades for classes he barely attended, gifts and money
from grateful alumni, a steady supply of girls, and so on.

But at six foot four, Jesse was too short for the pros. Jesse
graduated from college with a degree in physical education
and little else. Suddenly, he was just another unemployed
jock. He went into an emotional tailspin. Without the team,

the coach, the alumni, and the adoring fans, he felt like he was nothing, a has-been, a zero. He had no identity. He felt lost.

Identity in Stress and Distress

While most of us will never have to face an identity plunge as dramatic as Jesse's — from hero status to oblivion in only a few short months — we will, indeed, suffer our own identity crisis if we base our self-worth only on what we do. For example:

- What happens to the self-image of a woman who devotes her entire time to being super-mom when her kids grow up and leave home?
- How about the macho man who develops arthritis and diabetes and who can't be macho anymore?
- Or the workaholic who gets laid off?
- Or the glamour girl who gets old?

Why do co-dependents end up building their identity from the outside in? Well, when you consider the fact that their normal identity development has been interrupted, and that they are separated from themselves, it isn't difficult to see how they might not know who they really are.

At first avoidance of the real self, the true feelings and thoughts, is a realistic choice for the child in a troubled family. Avoidance becomes a tool they use to protect themselves from real and imagined threats to their well-being. Because of the rules that encourage the denial of self and because of the lack of trusted adult role models, the child sees no other choice.

For adult children co-dependents, the inability to communicate openly and honestly is clearly the result of a long adherence to the "no talk" rules. These dysfunctional and oppressive rules in combination form an iron curtain behind which the real self is hidden.

As a consequence, the adult child develops a pseudo-self, a self that consists of a set of sophisticated maneuvers and strategies that are designed to ensure survival.

Learning how to look the part and play the role requires a lot of time and energy. Developing the "right" image by wearing the right clothes, acting the right way or saying the right thing becomes almost second nature to the co-dependent. Trying to learn the rules of the game while mimicking the behavior of others gradually develops into a chronic preoccupation with trying to look normal.

Looking Good vs. Being Real

This co-dependent "looking good" psychology is really nothing more than the reflection of a false identity based on doing whatever the script tells you is the "right thing to do." Being true to yourself is not a part of being co-dependent.

Looking good is a show, a cosmetic cover-up, a posture. Playing the imposter means that the co-dependent must always live with a nagging fear that one day they will be found out. This nagging fear forces the co-dependent to scramble around even more in an effort to keep up the image. In time, what began as a simple means to survive develops into a harmful dependency on the rules of a sick co-dependent game.

These rules tell the co-dependent things like: "You should always know where you have been and where you are going. You should never be lost."

Of course, the reality for a co-dependent is that they are very often lost, even though they believe they aren't, even thought they sincerely believe they know what they're doing.

They're lost, all right: Lost in the shuffle of a dysfunctional script.

Some co-dependents spend their entire lives acting as though they understand and know what they're doing when they really don't, when they're really faking it. Choosing to fake it means that one must learn to cope with the free-floating anxiety that comes from living a lie.

Why be anxious? Because someone might see through the

co-dependent deception, someone might find out that you really don't know, or worse, that you really are confused and lost. So the co-dependent must continue to put a lot of energy into keeping up the facade in an effort to con themselves and others into believing that they really are in control of their lives.

The cumulative effect of this co-dependent lifestyle of anxious pretense and personal fraudulence inevitably destroys our ability to be open, to be childlike and needy. It denies us the freedom to ask important questions about those things that we don't really understand, or to express the thoughts and feelings that we need to express. So the co-dependent lives in an information vacuum, a vacuum that we fill with fear, shame and anxiety. Instead of really growing through our experiences we learn to perform and fake it. We become reactors instead of responders in life.

For me, the pressure to perform started very early in life. I remember thinking in kindergarten, "I gotta do good here. I mean real good." It was as if there was someone standing behind me looking over my shoulder and muttering, "You never know when this might show up on a transcript. Be sure to use those primary colors, and stay between the lines. It could be the difference between college and vo-tech." College, of course, was the place where you had to be, in order to be okay as a Subby.

Let's say you're a five or six-year-old kid growing up in an alcoholic family and listening to your parents screaming at each other, and wondering how you were going to survive when Mom and Dad got a divorce — which, of course, would be your fault. Stuff like this scares the hell out of a kid. So for 15 years I was haunted by the question: "Are we going to be a family or not?"

Now it's not normal under those conditions to expect a child to go to school and perform at an "A" level. But I did go to school, of course. And I came back with my less than perfect report cards, and my father would say to me, "Bob, I don't understand this B in math; I don't understand this C in English. You've got all the talent God could give anybody."

Then he'd say, "Why aren't you living up to your potential?" As if I could really get a handle on that question. I came to hate it whenever anyone talked about my great unfulfilled potential.

My father's a doctor, a physician. He's got his M. Deity. And my mother went to a school where they gave — get this — double "A"s. So when I'd get a good grade, my mother would say, "Yeah, that's nice. But when I went to school, there were some teachers who would give us two "A"s.

Naturally I never got the double "A" in a subject like Mom had. I couldn't have gotten that kind of a grade even if I'd wanted to. I remember going to my teacher one day and asking "Do you ever give two 'A's for really, really good stuff?"

He thought I was nuts.

In effect, I couldn't make the grade, so like any normal child surviving in a troubled co-dependent family, I learned to fake it in other ways. The child learns to develop a super red-alert warning system, a kind of psychological radar that sweeps a 500-yard radius. A radar that is on full 24-hour red alert.

Hyper-vigilant co-dependents are preoccupied with watching everything from the sidelines, trying to pick up cues about what's expected before entering the game. As an adult child, Normal meant being what others expected me to be. I'd scrutinize and study every situation looking for signs of what was expected, looking for cues that would help me be what you wanted me to be, or needed me to be. Hyper-alert and ever-vigilant, I spent a lot of time looking outward, scanning the territory. I didn't spend much time scanning the inner territory. I was a stranger to others, to be sure, but most of all I was a stranger to myself.

The Legislated Lifestyle

Some co-dependent folks, despite their rigid and close-minded adherence to the rules or to traditions, seem to be living perfectly contented lives. So it would be unfair to assume that all co-dependent people are necessarily dissatisfied or unhappy. What might be fair to assume is that these people are living a kind of narrow *legislated lifestyle*.

In a legislated lifestyle, there is clear dependency on the rules, but there are often no serious consequences as a result.

Certain religions and cultures, for example, may be very rigid and yet despite this fact those adults who live within these restrictive boundaries seem to be and often report that they are in fact living full, happy lives. How the children growing up in these systems are experiencing life is yet another question. What is good for one person may not always necessarily be good for another. Only time will tell. Today it is perfectly clear to me that there are many people who choose to live in a legislated lifestyle and are satisfied with their choice.

Take, for example, a man who has lived his whole life by the Golden Rule, "Live and Let Live." And despite all the stories of a past filled with turmoil and loss this man reports being content and attributes his serenity to this simple philosophy. What makes him tick, how does he really feel, or what does he really think? — all this remains a mystery to his family. "We don't know him," they report. Nonetheless, by all the external measures — a long successful career, a fifty-year marriage, two homes in retirement, and the father of three grown children — it would be naive to suggest that this man's simple philosophy of life had not served him well. If it works, why fix it?

While some might judge this man's approach to life as

lackluster or absent of emotional vitality, I believe it would be wrong to criticize him for his beliefs, particularly in light of how this simple and uncomplicated philosophy has carried him successfully across some eighty years of life.

The thought comes, "But how much more this man might have experienced, if . . ." However, such judgments are easy to make in retrospect. In recovery, we learn the true meaning of "Live and let live" as it pertains to our own lives, and to let go and relieve ourselves of the burden of judging others. In this process we also learn that we have the right to live as we choose.

As a closing note to this section on legislated lifestyles, consider the story of Diane, who I met at a conference several years ago. After I had given a talk on co-dependency and adult children, Diane came up to me and introduced herself. "I come from a strict military family," she said, "and my parents did everything by the book. We never talked about problems or feelings. We never questioned the authority of my parents, and I have never questioned the rightness or possible wrongness of this very legislated lifestyle. I look back now and realize that there were experiences that could have been handled differently."

Diane took a deep breath and continued, "What I want to know is this: Are you saying that I have to change who I am now because of this history?"

"Not at all," I replied. "Because you identify with this kind of family history and recognize it today as a legislated lifestyle, does not mean that you are not okay. If you're happy with your life and at peace with your family history, then why in God's name would you choose to upset your life by wrongly judging the past. You have every right to and every reason to live as you believe. I would only want you to know that you have the right to change if you feel that your past is getting in the way of your future."

In summary, those who come from a legislated lifestyle do not automatically pass into the world with "LOSER" stamped across their forehead. Being from a legislated lifestyle does not identify you as an adult child or as a person who will not find wholeness in life. I am only questioning the internalization of such a lifestyle as a way to avoid the conflicts of life.

Victims? Or Volunteers?

So where do we draw the line between what is a healthy dependency on the rules and what is an unhealthy co-dependent adherence to them?

For me, the answer to this question depends on several key issues:

First, and foremost, is the matter of free choice. That is to say, is the individual truly free to choose their own path?

Certainly, the issue of free choice is not a simple one to define, yet in the case of co-dependency, I believe it goes without saying that there is a clear difference between the freedom of choice for children and the freedom of choice for members of the adult population.

Since I firmly believe that co-dependency involves freedom of choice I would say without reservation that children, lacking the freedom of choice, must not be viewed as people suffering from co-dependency, but rather as people who are merely surviving.

From this vantage point I reach only one conclusion: **that co-dependency is an adult issue that develops as a result of one's conscious or unconscious choice to violate themselves by going against what they believe to be intuitively right, honest or most correct.**

Whether the co-dependency of one's adult life has its roots in a troubled childhood or more current struggle, it is within the assumption of adult free choice that the individual can no longer be seen as merely a victim of circumstances, but rather must be recognized as a co-dependent volunteer.

All things considered, I would say that it is the voluntary surrender of free choice as an adult that marks an individual's passage into co-dependency.

As difficult as this situation is for us, we must accept the fact that we have consciously or unconsciously surrendered our free choice before we can truly begin to recover from this cunning, baffling and powerful disease that has ruled over our lives.

Despite the very real potential of rejection, abandonment, loss or failure that may accompany our choices and despite our sometimes obvious lack of choice-making experience, we are nonetheless free agents who are responsible for making choices about how we will live.

Next, I ask, what are the consequences of living according to the rules? If the consequences violate another's rights or if the practices related to the rules diminish life in any way for those involved, then I say the rules are dysfunctional and the lifestyle self-limiting. In other words, any lifestyle that restricts freedom of choice, or in some way prevents self-actualization is likely to create a dysfunctional co-dependent reaction to life.

In the classic sense, co-dependency is the result of a conscious or unconscious denial and abandonment of self.

PART FIVE

Co-dependency:
The Concept and the Disease

Chapter 9

The Concept
of Co-dependency

I believe at this point in the discussion it would be useful to define co-dependency as both a concept and a disease. Of course, I realize, that in order to do this I will have to talk out of both sides of my mouth. I trust you understand that there are two kinds of people who can best accomplish such a feat — a recovering alcoholic, co-dependent adult child, or a recovering alcoholic, co-dependent adult. Given that I qualify as a member of this distinguished but humble group, the following represents my best effort at describing this somewhat confusing two-dimensional perspective of co-dependency.

To understand the conceptual framework of co-dependency it is important that one understand, at least in basic terms, what role our social, cultural, political and religious history has played in setting the stage for co-dependency.

To me, the social family and its rules serve as the foundation upon which all of us base our lives. Our values, attitudes and beliefs are all shaped by these external forces. From this perspective it is not beyond reason to suggest that our nuclear families are little more than a mini-reflection of those outside realities — a microcosmic representation of the larger external social family.

If, to take it a step further, we believe that our family and

the rules upon which our family operates are in fact a reflection of the larger social family, then it is logical to assume
that we ourselves are in part a mini-reflection of our social,
cultural, political and religious foundations. **Conceptually
speaking, co-dependency is a reality born out of the
combined influences of our social, cultural, political,
religious and nuclear family.**

Obviously, it is *not* true within these five dimensions of
our human family that only the dysfunctional rules of co-
dependency are being practiced. However, many of them
are.

How these now-identified rules of co-dependency first
came into being is, I believe, largely a consequence of our
austere psycho-social history. Consider how it might have
been to live a hundred years or so ago. Back then basic
survival and the meeting of these basic life needs would
certainly have consumed most of our ancestors' time. The
mere preoccupation with survival would have made asking
the question, "Who am I?" sound like so much self-indul-
gent crap. There would have been little time to dwell on
such non-productive issues, and even less inclination to
mull over the burden of questions like:

How do I feel?
Is there a God?
What's the meaning of life?

Imagine surviving the loss of your entire family as a result
of plague or war. Do you think that this type of experience
might be too overwhelming for you to face? And under
conditions that existed back then, do you think that in
order to survive this trauma you might not just shut down
emotionally?

Think of the plagues that rolled over Europe and deci-
mated half the population. What would be a natural emotional reaction to hearing the heavy carts roll through the
streets while the driver shouted "Bring out your dead!"
Numbness. A hollow impassiveness. A fatal stoicism.

This kind of history might very well have given cause for
a whole culture to shut down emotionally. From such a

From our world family to our own intra-personal family the rules of the system play a significant role in the process of identity development and recovery. The rules will either promote or undermine these processes. Much depends on how we choose to exercise them.

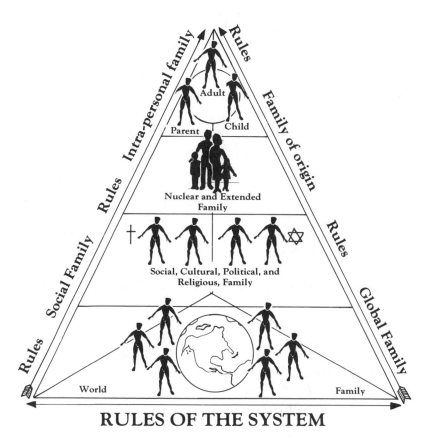

RULES OF THE SYSTEM

For the co-dependent individual recovery of the intra-personal family is of primary importance.

point in history on, it could have very well become the norm not to show your feelings. If you can't express your feelings, then why even have them?

In this light, passing along a "no talk" rule from generation to generation seems totally within the realm of possibility.

Once these rules, which in a clear sense have nothing at all to do with our current history, are passed on, they become dysfunctional and an inappropriate part of our contemporary social family. These rules have survived and reached out, laying the cold, dead hand of the past on the present reality.

No one seems to know why we as a culture practice these rules, but we follow them nonetheless. Rules that at one time served the common good and the collective purpose of SURVIVAL now diminish the common good and obstruct our search for meaning and identity.

To escape the fallout of our history requires that we challenge these antiquated rules which no longer serve the common good of humankind. With all the miracle drugs and creature comforts of our technological age many of us have arrived at a time when the quest for self-actualization is no longer a senseless waste of valuable time.

Co-dependency is a *pro-active disease* in which yesterday's learnings, attitudes, beliefs and rules interfere with today's learning, development and growth. And the rules of the system are the primary transmitting mechanism in the passage of co-dependency from one generation to the next.

As a society, as a family or as individuals, in order to know ourselves and reach our full potentials, we must first break through the dysfunctional co-dependent traditions of our past history. For those of us who have been afforded the opportunities of this new age, the pursuit of self-actualization is more than a luxury. It's a responsibility.

If in a metaphorical sense we think of the collective family of man as a single being, then even beyond the psychosocial "concept" of co-dependency we might begin to see how the "disease" of co-dependency could have literally entered into the collective spirit of our social family and interfered with its innate need to evolve and grow. You and I, our families, and our society are all systems that need to be free to evolve.

Short of taking this metaphorical image or analogy too literally, I would nonetheless venture to say that co-dependency and its basic structure is more than just a concept rooted in social history, it is also a cultural disease. A disease transmitted across the generations through the blind adherence to rules that no longer make sense.

Co-dependency is a disease of the intra-personal system. Body, mind and spirit are divided from one another as a result of the dysfunctional rules.

Chapter 10

The Disease
of Co-dependency

To begin with, it is necessary to define disease (or
dis-ease) in terms that distinguish it as something other than
only a biological or genetic disorder. The dictionary definition of disease goes something like this:

Disease: An *abnormal condition of an organism or part,
especially as a consequence of infection, inherent weakness,
or environmental stress, that impairs the normal physiologi-
cal functioning.*

In light of this definition, what do I mean when I say that
co-dependency is a dis-ease? First of all, I believe that co-dependency becomes a disease when as a result of prolonged
exposure to, or practice of, dysfunctional rules (ie, don't
discuss problems, don't talk about feelings, don't rock the
boat, etc.) the individual internalizes the practice of these
rules in an effort to manage their unresolved emotional
conflicts, and by doing so interrupts their own normal emotional, psychological and social growth.

*Unconsciously, the individual moves beyond the simple
manipulations of or management of external forces through*

CO-DEPENDENCY:

Is an emotional, behavioral, and psychological pattern of coping which develops as a result of prolonged exposure to and practice of a dysfunctional set of family rules. In turn, these rules make difficult or impossible the open expression of thoughts and feelings. Normal identity development is thereby interrupted.

In essense co-dependency is the reflection of a delayed identity development.

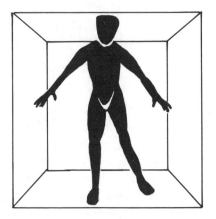

adherence to the rules and has begun to manage and control the internal realities as well.

In this regard, the rules represent "environmental stress" — which eventually translates into internal stress. As things progress, the individual becomes increasingly dependent on the practice of these same rules in order to manage the otherwise "normal" emotional, behavioral and psychological discomfort of the co-dependent experience.

If we assume that an otherwise healthy pattern of coping existed in the first place, then it is the ultimate internalization of these dysfunctional rules that separates the individual from himself and so creates a disease of the body, mind and spirit. In short, the internalization of these dysfunctional co-dependent rules interfere with what should have been a "normal" or "healthy" development into a clear and autonomous adult identity.

Thus a distinction can be made between early onset co-dependency and late onset co-dependency. In early onset co-dependency, a person develops an adult co-dependent lifestyle as a result of having grown up under a set of dysfunctional rules in a troubled family. Early onset co-dependents come from alcoholic families, emotionally ill families, physically or sexually abusive families or rigid, fundamentalistic families.

In contrast, the late onset co-dependent is a person who does not have a troubled family history, but who gets into a troubled relationship or a troubled family as an adult and begins to comply with the dysfunctional rules of that relationship or family.

The majority of co-dependent folks are early onset. Of course, there are exceptions to every rule, but generally speaking, adult children are always co-dependents, but co-dependents are not always adult children.

While the treatment needs and recovery issues will often vary greatly between these two types of co-dependency, the core issue remains the same — the rules are dysfunctional, and the normal development and growth have been hindered as a result of them.

Identity development is a lifetime process, and so can be interrupted at any time.

THE PROGRESSION
OF CO-DEPENDENCY

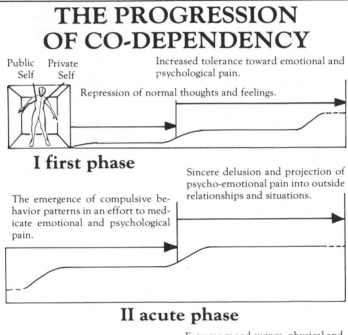

Public   Private
Self   Self

Increased tolerance toward emotional and psychological pain.

Repression of normal thoughts and feelings.

I first phase

The emergence of compulsive behavior patterns in an effort to medicate emotional and psychological pain.

Sincere delusion and projection of psycho-emotional pain into outside relationships and situations.

II acute phase

Psychosomatic symptomatology may begin to surface. (i.e., migraines, chest pains, lower back pain and insomnia). Compulsive behavior patterns may become more obsessive.

Extreme mood swings, physical and emotional breakdown, severe depression and thoughts of suicide are common in this stage of co-dependency.

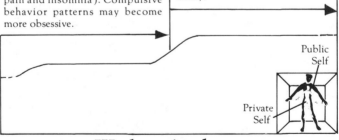

Public
Self

Private
Self

III chronic phase

The longer we live according to a co-dependent script the further we drift away from ourselves. The further we drift, the more anxiety and emotional pain we feel. This progression continues to worsen until we break out of our dysfunctional co-dependent mold.

My Fam-Damily Legacy

Like most people, my hindsight is 20-20 and so it seems obvious to me now that from the beginning I was set up by the dysfunctional rules of my family to be a co-dependent. Of course, it wasn't until my early thirties that I really began to look at my life or question my family history. Until that time I simply followed the rules of my family like the good little boy that I was.

The past was past, I said to myself. "No sense in crying over spilt milk." And besides, real men — and healthy recovering alcoholics — should Let Go and Let God.

I understand now that the dis-ease I felt inside was the result of the many years of denial and avoidance of myself, my history and all that went with it. I had learned to repress all those unpleasant thoughts and feelings associated with my childhood. Back then denying the true me made good sense, and besides, as a child how was I to know that the expression of real thoughts and feelings was necessary to becoming a whole person?

Well, the apple falls not far from the tree, as they say, and I was like all children destined in part to be what I was taught to be.

How many of us were fortunate enough as children to see our parents or other adults around us face into emotional conflict without assaulting one another, running away or just sitting like a bump on a log.

When I was growing up in my alcoholic family, I never saw my parents really work through their conflicts. I saw them make it through crisis, after crisis, but exactly how they made it was never clear. To me, it seemed as though they either stuffed what was going on, or they over-reacted to it.

As I grew older, I felt like the best policy was to avoid conflict, whatever it might be. On the other hand, once I had run out of tolerance for whatever the reason, I would over-react. I was like a car that had two speeds: Reverse and full speed ahead. A real Dr. Jekyll and Mr. Hyde personality.

In either case the end result was the same: I lost the respect of others, and I lost respect for myself. I recognize now that going into a conflict — in particular a relationship conflict — I had no healthy model to draw from. My only choices were those I had learned in childhood, the rules I had taken to heart and remembered.

I learned there was a set of rigid rules that said there were certain things you did in functioning as part of this system in order to make it. And if you didn't do what you were supposed to do, you got into trouble. Nobody tells you that if you do the wrong thing, you're going to be punished. You find out when you've done the wrong thing *because* you get punished. In situations where there was conflict, I learned there are two safe ways to go: Over-reaction or no reaction at all. Over-reaction is a safe out because it indicates to others that in a sense you're out of control, you've passed the point of no return, so they often retreat from the conflict. It's safe because while you're getting all caught up in your new reactive episode, you don't have to be with yourself or the consequence.

Under-reaction or passivity is safe because you can simply numb yourself to the conflict and by doing so manage to erect a facade of invulnerability and indifference that seems to say: "Nothing is bothering me."

My model for dealing with conflict was my parents' model for dealing with conflict. And I believed that model was crazy. My mother would over-react and my father would go passive. Between my over-reacting and my passive avoidance I must have looked pretty damned insane. My parents sure did.

And this was only part of a whole constellation of ineffective and destructive coping skills I learned while growing up in my co-dependent family.

I know my parents weren't intentionally trying to hurt me, but as it is, I need to understand that they did hurt me. No, they did not totally fail to provide for me. Obviously if they had, I would not be here. Nonetheless a necessary part of recovery is for us to gain a balanced perspective of those who raised us. We need to lift the veils of denial from our eyes and see the past as it was, not as we wish it might have been.

Just because our parents were co-dependents themselves does not absolve them from their responsibilities as parents anymore than being drunk excuses one from the responsibility for hurting someone while driving under the influence.

But because blaming and being angry with one's parents often creates guilt and touches on our shame, we stop ourselves from looking into our real thoughts and feelings about them. I know this from first-hand experience. I remember how many times I felt the call to run to the defense of my parents whenever I heard someone criticize what they had done. I would say things like:

"At the time, they did the best they could with the tools they had."

Certainly this was true, but there was no real need for me to defend them in the first place. I realize now that it was just one of those co-dependent responses I used to avoid looking at my own true feelings.

Moreover, I understand as an adult child, blaming myself or others was easier than blaming my folks. Yes, my parents certainly did make mistakes. And, yes, I certainly did need to work through my bad feelings about them. But in the end it was myself and my own shame that I really needed to face. I didn't know back then that my anger and blaming of others was a symptom of my shame.

Thou Shalt Not Share

For me, getting through the blaming stage of my recovery from co-dependency meant that I had to start from where I was. And where I was in the beginning was angry at my folks.

Convinced as I was that feeling the way I did about my parents was wrong and that blaming them was even worse, I had lots of sleepless nights worrying about what might happen if I broke with the long-standing co-dependent tradition of silence.

Don't talk!

What would happen if I broke the silence? Would I lose my family altogether? Would I be rejected by my A.A. group? Would I lose control of myself?

Breaking the rules seemed like such a foolish thing to do. Talking about my feelings before had never seemed to help, so what good would it do to start now? Everything I thought and felt told me to keep my mouth shut and just try to forget about it.

The anxiety I felt about talking to anyone about my feelings was bad enough and the anxiety about confronting my family was more than I thought I could bear. Fortunately, I was not alone in my crisis. I had a sponsor in A.A. who intuitively understood what I was going through. He told me that I was capable of facing my fears and that what I had to do was a normal part of growing up. He helped me see that being true to myself was the only way to continue my recovery.

Most important of all, he helped me to recognize that *what others might do in response to my sharing was not as important as why I was sharing with them in the first place.* He taught me that there was an intrinsic healing quality in respectful and responsible sharing. He taught me to share for what it would do for me and not for what I expected it would get me from others.

As a co-dependent I had built my whole existence around following the rules and worrying about what others would think of me. I didn't know that sharing for my own sake would do me any good. In the past, my sharing with others had more to do with how they would respond, than it did with what my sharing would do for me.

I had heard for years that recovery was a selfish program, but I had never before understood what this meant. What I thought was that being selfish was wrong. I didn't know that sometimes selfishness is a good thing.

Well, I started doing some of that selfish sharing and I started to learn how I had abandoned myself by giving others the power to make me or break me. As a child I had been the victim of whatever shortcomings my parents might have had, but as an adult I had become a volunteer.

It was difficult to face myself and accept that my parents were no longer responsible for the on-going problems in my life. And by comparison to this painful awakening, I would say that the task of facing my parents, which I eventually did, was but a small part of my journey back to myself.

I have faced the enemy, and the enemy was me. Having had this "spiritual awakening", I would have to say that for the child who is forced to grow up in a troubled family under a set of dysfunctional rules, the development of survivorship skills must be viewed as a normal emotional, behavioral, and psychological response to stress. Under certain conditions, such as being a child in a troubled family where no real power of choice exists, survival must *never* be viewed as dysfunctional or co-dependent.

Thus, the adult child co-dependent can say that as a child they were acting normally under the circumstances, and that they were only doing what they had to do to survive. On the other hand, as adults we are no longer the victim but the volunteer. This being the case, the confusion that adult children experience and the loneliness that they feel, including the fear of intimacy and abandonment are all normal adult consequences of a troubled childhood. In short, it is the history and not the child who is at fault.

Moreover, from this perspective of co-dependency we can also begin to recognize that our parents are not the only source of our pain. Not that we don't have reason to feel angry with them about the past, but more importantly that in the unfolding process of recovery, we ultimately come to recognize that it is the parent and adult models that we carry inside who are responsible for our on-going co-dependent struggles.

Many of us left home, defiantly vowing, "I'll never do it like my parents." Unfortunately, we are what we learn, and eventually, somehow, our parents manage to take up residence inside us. Only later as adults do we discover that we have never truly left home. In fact, in many ways we are just like our parents, who played the same game, different name — yet all products of a co-dependent heritage, "Lost in the shuffle."

Chapter 11

Shame —
The Core of Co-dependency

As children we are developmentally and constitutionally incapable of understanding that our parents may be sick. We don't see that their sickness is the reason they do the things they do or say the things they say. We experience the neglect, the abandonment, the verbal, sexual, and physical abuse, but we don't understand it — we don't see the sick co-dependent logic that fuels the abusiveness of our parents.

Just as a malfunctioning nuclear reactor releases invisible radioactivity into the air, so the troubled co-dependent family system also produces a kind of harmful fallout that seeps into and upsets the delicate emotional and psychological balance of its children.

As children, all we know is how we feel, and if what our parents do or say hurts us, then we end up believing that perhaps they meant to hurt us — which hurts us even more. Because we can't understand what's going on, as children we may decide that in some way we are responsible for the way our parents act.

If we choose to believe the latter, and we often do, then in time we will as children come to believe that there is something profoundly wrong with who we are. Not just that we have done something wrong — this is guilt — but rather that we are somehow innately bad and therefore responsible for all the problems in the family — which is our ingrained sense of shame.

This private logic — that there is something fundamentally wrong with us — is the cornerstone of a shame-based, co-dependent lifestyle.

Gradually we begin to judge in a negative way all those thoughts and feelings that run contrary to the way in which we believe we should think and feel. There are many conflicting and inconsistent rules that cause us to become even more confused, anxious and ashamed. For example — "Be happy!" *But don't be happy when others around you are unhappy.*

Or: "Be honest!" *But don't say anything that might cause discomfort or pain for someone else.*

Because a child is unable to resolve these intellectual emotional double-binds, they learn to mistrust themselves and others. As adults these unresolved emotional conflicts continue to undermine the foundation of trust. Without trust, change of any kind becomes a threat to our sense of security.

While change — even positive change — is often frightening for almost everyone, the mere thought of change can literally immobilize the adult child with fear and anxiety. Like little children afraid of the dark, adult co-dependents fall victim to their own imaginary fears. These imaginary fears, in turn, continue to be reinforced by the practice of the rules that lie beneath them. Even the most basic decisions about when to eat or which movie to go see become major obstacles because of our fear of making mistakes. Eventually this confusing and conflicting co-dependent system of logic turns into fear of fear.

The longer we live in this co-dependent state of fear and anxiety, the more rigid and myopic we become in our efforts to manage the internal stress by controlling the external realities of our world.

Managing the outcome, being in control of things —these behaviors are the essence of a co-dependent's efforts to relieve the free-floating anxiety over the nagging division between the real self and the self we pretend to be.

There may be numerous ways that a co-dependent person would endeavor to maintain control over his anxiety, but it seems clear to me that in the majority of cases, this need to overcontrol or hyper-manage is based on a deep-seated shame that to feel confused, lost, or out of control — even occasionally — is wrong.

Beneath this layer of erroneous logic that *the normal and occasional inability to control the internal and external realities of life* is wrong lies the even deeper foundation of the mistaken logic of shame that says: "I am a wrong person, no good, defective and imperfect."

Like a sliver that works its way deep into the flesh and later becomes infected, the private shame and mistaken logic of a child's troubled past festers on into adulthood, creating an infection of co-dependent anxiety.

To me this central core of shame and mistaken logic is the notion that despite our innocence as children, we come to judge ourselves as intrinsically wrong and bad. At the core of our lives we are ashamed — ashamed of our past, ashamed of our lives, ashamed of ourselves — our thoughts and actions, our whole personhood.

Once this core of shame infects our lives, even the simplest of mistakes will be translated into evidence of our basic imperfection:

"I can't ever do anything right!"
"I always seem to screw things up!"

The child growing up in a troubled family becomes the innocent victim of circumstance.

I don't believe that any rational adult would think to blame a child for the way their parents act. Yet this is exactly what the adult child co-dependent does to himself. For some of us this tendency to blame ourselves for the trouble in our family is fostered by vivid memories of our parents, siblings or other adult caregivers telling us that we are, in fact, the cause for all the problems.

Take for example statements like: "Things were fine around here before you were born." Or: "You're the reason why Mom and Dad are always fighting."

Consider the story of Ben, a 35-year-old attorney, who struggled for years with the searing memory of his mother's drunken rages. Once when he was still in grade school she cornered him, grabbed him by the shoulders and hissed: "Things were fine around here before you were born! Your father and I were happy."

"What did I know?" says Ben, in retrospect. "I thought she was right, and if she was right, then I was wrong. I mean, my whole existence was wrong. So when my parents finally got divorced, no one had to spell it out for me. I was the reason. Not the drinking, not the mental abuse or emotional cruelty, but me. If only I had never been born they would still be happy and still be married."

Obviously, the internalization of such mistaken logic can be extremely damaging to a child's self-image and their relationship to the rest of the world. It's a weighty responsibility for a child to see himself as the sole cause of other people's problems. Needless to say, this kind of mistaken logic didn't do a thing for Ben's self-esteem.

Jan, another adult child, once told me that her mother used to tell her that she was a bad seed. As a child, Jan said that she was never sure exactly what her mother meant by this but she always felt somehow that it meant that she was a bad person. In light of all the stories I have heard, stories just like Ben's and Jan's, I know that children are vulnerable and that abuse in this form can leave deep and permanent scars.

The Importance of Memory

For other co-dependent adult children, the past is like a dark hole where clear memories are difficult to find. In these cases, the lack of memory is usually due to a combination of factors.

In other instances denial and repression of painful memories prevent us from being able to recall the past. We are like deep-sea divers scanning murky waters. Now and then we catch little glimpses of the past, but overall we are groping blindly in the dark. We can't quite get the light to focus, and even if we did, we really don't want to go any deeper for fear we might not like what we find.

As the legends on old maps used to read, "Terra incognita. Here there be monsters."

In still other instances the lack of childhood memories may be due to the mere routine of abuse, abandonment or neglect. In these cases, the adult child simply develops a tolerance for the intolerable. Why should there be any particularly painful or traumatic recollection when the history of abuse — be it overt or covert in nature — was merely a way of life? If such things are experienced too long, they end up being taken for granted. If this happens, then perspective is lost and without something to compare our experience with, it becomes easy to simply overlook an otherwise troubled past. In some cases, there are utterly no memories of good or bad.

If every morning you woke up to the consistency of inconsistency, or if you lived every day in an emotional vacuum where nothing new or special ever happened — what a trap! — it might not be long before no day would seem all that different from any other. You might just end up comfortably numb. There are no memories, good or bad, because nothing stands out.

The loss of childhood memories or the lack of them says, by itself, something significant about one's childhood.

Healthy memories are a cushion for sanity, and without them we are left to guess about what is normal and sane.

PART SIX

Issues in Recovery

Chapter 12

Identity

The Gift of Recovery

Recovery is not likely to begin with a personal visit from God. Nor is it likely that prayer alone would bring about a spontaneous remission from co-dependency. There are no short-cuts or quick fixes. Recovery is a process that takes time, hard work and a willingness to change. Proverbial wisdom reminds us that God helps those who help themselves, and so it is with recovery from co-dependency.

Personally, I have no doubt that God listens to our prayers. And my experience tells me that more often than not, those prayers are answered, one way or another, through other people or situations that come into our lives and lead us into a *process* of change which will bring us back to ourselves.

Unfortunately, most co-dependents are frightened by change — even positive change. As a result they are at best reluctant recipients of the gift of recovery.

Clearly, recovery depends on change, yet having to change means having to risk losing control — losing control over our feelings, our relationships, our lives. Unable to face the fear of losing control, the co-dependent often retreats into a defensive game of rationalization that says,

- "I can't let anyone see that I'm floundering or in distress."

- "I can't allow anyone to see that I'm lost."
- "I can't let anyone know that I need help."
- "I can't admit that I'm wrong or that others are right."

In effect, we are saying, "I must turn my back on the gift of recovery because . . ."

. . . Because if I open myself up, if I let my guard down, then people will see me as weak, vulnerable and incompetent. Inwardly the co-dependent fervently prays for help, but when it comes, they won't accept it. It's like we want some medicine, we want some relief, but when the medicine comes — yuuuk! — it doesn't taste right, so we won't take it. It's a classical approach-avoidance conflict.

We want help, but we want it the way we want it, and always on our own terms. We want the short course or the quick fix. Like a child unable to face their problems directly, the co-dependent resorts to manipulation and indirect methods to get their needs met.

When co-dependents come to me for counseling, usually for something other than for themselves, they often start out by saying, "I'm here to get some help for my children."

I say, "More important than your children, I need to hear about you first."

Still dodging, they say, "Well there are some concerns I have about my husband."

"No," I tell them, "I don't need to know about your husband right now either. I need to know about you."

This kind of pre-therapeutic sparring and jousting is a typical but sophisticated co-dependent game. I call it Trivial Dispute, and the object of the game is to evade the confrontations and avoid having to deal with the real issue, "Me."

Co-dependents would rather talk about almost anything but themselves — the kids, the relatives, the weather. And for good reason. Because they feel ashamed. Beneath the gamesmanship of Trivial Dispute there is almost always a co-dependent player who is running away from the core of their shame, which is the inner script that says, "I don't like me."

Worst of all, in many cases the co-dependent doesn't even have an inkling of who they really are. So in a very real sense, there isn't even a "who" to like or dislike.

It's harder for the co-dependent to become a real person, because they tend to operate out of a shame-based logic that is saying: "The only way to get love is to do what others think is The Right Thing." If your identity is solely bound up in someone else's truth or someone else's idea of what is right and proper, then, as I discussed earlier, you have an identity that is only skin deep.

The locus of control, the governor of our okayness, lies in the management of things outside ourselves.

The co-dependent motivation to do the right thing is this: "If I play the game right, then you're going to love me." My people-pleasing has a market value, and your acceptance and approval of me define my personhood. Consequently, the outcome of a co-dependent lifestyle usually turns out something like this:

- "I did all the right things, I was a good woman . . . so how did I end up married to such a jerk?"
- "I was a good hard and loyal worker, I gave my boss 15 years of my life, and then without warning, they replaced me with a computer. I thought I had some worth."

But true self-worth and security don't come from some external source. It comes from developing a solid and clear internal sense of self. Unfortunately, it's precisely this process of forming a secure internal sense of self that gets stunted in the dysfunctional family, where silence, secrecy and insanity reigns supreme.

In the truest sense, the co-dependent suffers from a delayed identity development syndrome. In the natural order of things, one's identity should mature and become clearer over time. Unfortunately, for the individual caught up in a co-dependent reality, the process of growth, change and the development are interrupted, if not blocked altogether.

Coming to know and love yourself is the ultimate gift in recovery.

CO-DEPENDENCY
adulthood

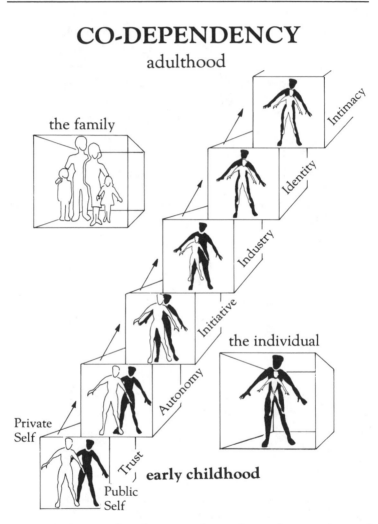

the family

the individual

Intimacy

Identity

Industry

Initiative

Autonomy

Private
Self

Trust

early childhood

Public
Self

Normal identity development depends on the practice and support of healthy family rules. The ascending boxes in this diagram represent Eric Erickson's first six stages of human development.

Chapter 13

Breaking the Silence

Breaking out of the silence of the alcoholic and the chemically dependent family — or any other dysfunctional system — is probably the most crucial step that co-dependents will have to take on the road to recovery.

Breaking the silence, however, doesn't mean unrestrained self-disclosure. It doesn't mean going around and ventilating our pain and pecadillos, our imagined crimes and misdemeanors, to just anyone who will listen.

What the co-dependent individual needs is to find a safe and healthy place to break the silence. A place where there are healthy rules and healthy people who can model healthy sharing. Call it a sanctuary. Sometimes divulging the whole truth and nothing but the truth so help you God is absolutely the worst thing to do. The consequences of too much random or impulsive honesty may end up making things worse instead of better.

I think there is a time and a place for everything, and sometimes the "don't talk" rule is a healthy edict to follow. But a model that shows us how to be open when we need to be open and a model that shows us how to be closed when we need to be closed is an important thing for the recovering co-dependent to find.

Inside my alcoholic family I didn't share, I didn't talk, and the accumulated layers of not talking about how I felt or what I thought turned my life into a pressure cooker. On top of this, I also learned all the co-dependent rules of the culture, which only served to further screw down the lid on my personal pressure cooker.

I was a walking bundle of nerves and when it came to finding relief from the pressure cooker, I turned to alcohol. When I found alcohol, I found instant relief: the lid came off and out rushed all the pressure. I was hooked from the first drink. How would I have done otherwise?

Drinking seemed like the logical choice. So what would a healthy person have done in my place? Back then I had no models to draw from, and my perspective was, to say the least, narrow.

I realize now that in order to hold onto our sanity or to model sanity for our children we must first possess the knowledge of free choice and the courage to exercise it. In the dysfunctional family, the rules often restrict the individual's freedom of choice and expression. Limited by this reality and the lack of healthy role models to follow, the individual is drawn into an insidious game of silence and denial of the real self. It boils down to one glaring principle:

If we lack the freedom to seek, then we lose our perspective. And if we lose our perspective, then it follows that we will also lose our sanity.

Many of us have been living for years within the silence of a co-dependent lifestyle. Inside this insane reality, we lack connectedness to others, to ourselves, and to our higher power. Consequently we lack the critical perspective that would offer us insight into our situation and give us direction. Until we break the silence that keeps us isolated, we will be unable to build the trusting relationships that we all need and long for.

No one recovers alone, and difficult though it may be, we must all break through the silence of our co-dependent histories and begin to develop those relationships that we lack. In order to do this we must take a leap of faith and join a new family, a new system — one that offers perspective and is held together by a fabric that promotes life, models wholeness and offers us hope.

If sanity, perspective, and recovery are all dependent on belonging to a healthy system that holds firmly to these values, then we must as part of our journey become willing to take a fearless and searching moral inventory of ourselves and the family system from whence we came.

The over-riding question is: "Does my family system promote life, model wholeness, and offer hope?" It's hard enough to know yourself, much less your family.

There have been times in recovery when I think I've discovered pieces of truth about my family and about what happened — even times of certainty about where I had been and where I was going — curious moments of awakening when I felt not lost but found. In those precious moments of awakening — and I believe we all get them from time to time — it becomes perfectly clear where you are. You feel truly oriented and somehow *right* — right with yourself and the world.

How many of us alone have been able to hang on to those moments for very long? Rapidly the God-given insights come, linger for a period and then slip away, hopefully to be rediscovered or re-invented . . .

In order to hold on to our insights, we need to share them and make an effort to lay a solid foundation of support upon which to grow and build a new life.

Of course, as I've discussed earlier, there is always an element of intoxication in being lost in the shuffle. However, in this culture there is little tolerance for being lost.

Sound familiar?

After all is said and done, the truth is that in this co-dependent culture you don't really have the right to be lost. For if you're lost and admit to it, there's a good chance that someone will up and say, "Well, what's your problem? Why aren't you on top of things? Why don't you know where the hell you're going? Get your act together and grow up!"

My father used to tell me how he prided himself on self-control, and how he took pride in others who did the same. I never heard my father say that expressing your feelings was a bad thing to do, but just the same, I never saw him do it. As a child I simply came to believe that showing your feelings was tantamount to losing control.

Consequently, as an adult it was very difficult for me to admit to my feelings. I was still a child inside trying to be like my father, a man who never lost control.

I remember on one particular occasion an AA sponsor of mine was listening to me give a talk about self-control. After I finished my talk, he came up to me and said, "Bob, everything you just said sounded like so much psychobabble."

Well, I was not about to admit that he was right, yet intuitively I knew that he was. I began to scramble around like some guy who had just jumped off a moving bus and was trying to keep from falling on his face. Before I could regain my composure, he hit again, this time with a question.

"Do you know how lost you sound, Bob?"

"Well," I admitted, "I'm just a little confused."

He said, "No, you're *lost*."

In an angry voice I blurted, "Okay, I'm *lost*. So what's your point?" (I always got defensive when I got caught.)

He told me, "You know, Bob, to know that you're lost is to know a lot."

Suddenly it struck me that to be lost is to be someplace. That possibility never occurred to me before. You see, I was always too busy trying to avoid the unpleasant, anxious and often embarrassing position of being lost.

Looking as though you're found. Translation: Faking it.

The structure of co-dependency stands on loose ground.

It's an unstable, shifty, and delusional facade. In the co-dependent world of appearances we can dress ourselves to look okay, we can cosmetically alter the life we've built with an external coating of material goods, college degrees, certificates of training and other stamps of approval. We can dress up for success and have our hair styled, drive a fancy car or wear expensive clothes with designer labels, but beneath it all it's still a body by Bondo. [See Part Four]

Living the script, hiding behind a facade, never challenging tradition, and playing it safe — these strategies lie at the heart of co-dependency. Controlled by phantoms of the past and unrealistic expectations of the future, the co-dependent is destined to fail. Despite the co-dependent's efforts to pound out the dents, sand down the rust and paint over the damage, the end product remains a Bondo-bodied automobile that can't be driven off the showroom floor.

So there you have it, a co-dependent Body by Bondo, a pseudo-identity, that won't hold up under normal stresses and strains of life, normal living conditions. Conditions like, say:

- Being married . . .
- Having children . . . (Think about that one)
- Building a career . . .
- Owning a home . . .
- Managing money . . .
- Practicing a faith . . .

Suddenly faced with the demands of an adult life, the co-dependent finds himself lost in the shuffle with no internal road map to follow. Even when confronted in a loving way, it is difficult for the co-dependent to accept help because they believe they should be able to handle things alone. They want to *appear* as though they are still in control, and that they know what is going on. It's not okay for them to fail.

Their lips start moving, they act as if things are fine, while inside they feel lost and ashamed. When a co-dependent fails, it's not like they just made an ordinary human mistake. Instead, they internalize their mistake and view It as more evidence that there is something "innately wrong" with them. After all, says the co-dependent logic of shame, "I shouldn't make mistakes in the first place and when I do, it's just another example of my flawed and imperfect nature."

God will surely punish me one day for all the terrible things I've done!

I've met lots of co-dependents who have told me things like they thought they'd lost a child because God was angry with them. Give me a break! To believe that God has nothing better to do than to keep a running inventory of your mistakes, matching sins with appropriate punishments is clearly a crazy and immature logic. Nonetheless, this is exactly the kind of logic that operates within the lives of so many co-dependents.

Co-dependents are divided spirits, imprisoned by feelings of shame, self-hate and self-doubt. Without support to break the silence and escape the hold of this dysfunctional co-dependent logic, there can be no recovery.

RECOVERY

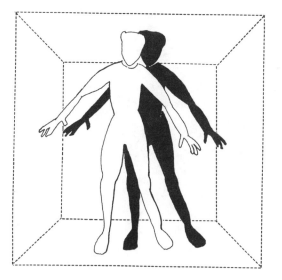

Recovery from co-dependency requires a balanced integration of the public and private self. The balance of these two dimensions of self depends on a healthy relationship between one intrapersonal family made up of our parent, our adult, and our child.

Chapter 14

Back to the Basics

When you're lost in the woods, survival means that you get back to the basics, heat, shelter, food, water and rest. When you get lost in life, the same principles apply. Somewhere along the way all those things that you've done, all those places you've been, and all those things that you heard, but never seemed to remember — one day, as you take the risk to break out of this silence, which is your first mission, all those pieces will somehow come together and have meaning. Recovery always seems to go this way. I don't know why, but I believe in the process of getting back to the basics.

Of course, our feelings are basic. I can remember when I was a child hearing my father say many times, "What does all this feeling stuff have to do with anything?" It's a question many people have asked in all seriousness.

Now I appreciate that feelings aren't always the most logical things, yet at the same time to deny your feelings altogether violates an older, more insistent logic: "If you don't talk about them, then you act them out."

So the fact that you have feelings isn't the problem. It's what you do with your feelings that really matters.. Recovery means finding a balance between logic and emotion. Building a healthy identity depends on our finding this balance.

Inside my alcoholic family we kept the lid on our feelings

and used our logic to handle whatever came up. We depended on our logic to control our feelings, and in the process we became sincerely deluded and emotionally numb.

If you asked me about my family, I would simply tell you a plausible lie. I didn't see my lying as a *lie*. I thought I was just being a good kid. I was loyal, I was keeping up appearances.

And so it goes. We talk about everything but what is really happening or how we really feel.

Being a member of a co-dependent family system meant that I *was* my family and my family *was me*. There were no boundaries and to me there was no difference. I was ashamed of my family, so I was ashamed of myself. I blamed my family, so I blamed myself. I didn't like my family, so I didn't like myself.

I don't like myself.

I believe this co-dependent self-loathing is a struggle for millions of people and lies at the heart of most mental health problems in this country. Problems like alcoholism, chemical dependency, workaholism, and eating disorders. Long range recovery from any of these addictive issues ultimately depends upon recovery from the underlying co-dependency and the imbalance between our public and private self.

In the language of Transactional Analysis (T.A.) recovery from co-dependency means building a balanced relationship between the Parent, the Adult and the Child that live within us. For the alcoholic, over-eater, bulimic or anorexic individual, we know that in order to treat the underlying co-dependency of their struggle, we first need to treat their primary addiction. Only then will the individual be able to employ their God-given abilities and face the unresolved co-dependent issues that divide them from themselves.

Repeat: First Things First

Again, let's be clear about one thing: **First things first.** *If someone who happens to be a co-dependent is addicted to alcohol, food or other drugs, the focus of treatment and personal recovery should begin by* **getting the addiction under control and becoming drug-free** *or* **abstinent.**

So you get drug-free, and you wonder when the serenity starts, and then the Old-Timer says, "Son, one of these days . . ."

And you say to yourself, "Hey, if I have to wait that long to have some serenity, I may just have to quit, drop out of recovery altogether." Because I want something quick, some temporary relief, a bit of instant gratification, or some short cut to serenity. If you're a co-dependent, chances are that postponement of gratification is not one of your strongest traits. Working a program of recovery means practicing patience one day at a time.

I didn't find any short cuts, and I don't believe you will either. I tried the hurry-up-and-get-well approach in AA. I rushed towards my Fifth Step, crashed and burned. I didn't come out of there feeling washed clean. Instead I came out of that experience feeling like Hulk Hogan had just given me a body slam.

I got in touch with the fact that I was really in trouble — trouble in my heart, trouble in my soul, trouble with my friends and worst of all, trouble with my recovery. I discovered that I was more than an alcoholic.

It was through this experience that I discovered that I was also a co-dependent. Because I no longer drank didn't mean that everything else in my life was going to get better automatically.

The thing that hit me right away in AA was the second step that said something about . . . *came to believe that a power greater than ourselves could restore us to sanity.* "I'm not insane," I told myself. And then there was the first step that

said that we were powerless and our lives were unmanage-
able.

I wasn't so concerned about recognizing the powerlessness and unmanageability of my situation as I was about the
idea that I had not been sane. After all, for so many years I
had carried off an act of okayness, that I think anyone who
didn't know me would have judged as rather sane.

People who saw me from afar would have said, "Bob's a
normal kind of guy. He's a 24-year-old man who's holding
down a good job, he's got a woman he's in love with. His
father's a doctor, his mother's a career woman. Why he
could get the *Gentleman's Quarterly* Stamp of Approval."

Sure he could.

Chapter 15

Sanity vs. Insanity

Everything looked SO good on the surface, but on the inside, things felt pretty crazy. Doubting my sanity became a big issue for me as I scrambled around in that cloud of confusion which I know now to be the typical co-dependent experience. I was a recovering alcoholic who was certain that his craziness and his drinking were one and the same. Consequently, I believed that if I stopped drinking, then my craziness would also stop.

Wrong again.

Today I see the underlying co-dependency of my addiction as the issue that always undermined the quality of my sobriety and left me feeling crazy. Still as a recovering alcoholic, I now also see myself as a recovering adult child co-dependent.

Getting in touch with my co-dependency was not an easy thing to do, particularly in my AA family, because at that time in history, alcoholics were not seen as co-dependent. But more than that: We just didn't talk about other issues in Alcoholics Anonymous. If you wanted to talk about something other than the Twelve Steps or staying sober, then you were expected to go see a counselor or a psychiatrist about those outside issues.

Co-dependency was at best an Al-Anon issue, and it had nothing to do with the main business of staying sober. Of course, we intuitively knew that to deny our feelings would eventually poison our sobriety and set ourselves up for a relapse. But the AA rules said "No," and emotional recovery was not discussed.

The irony was this: As practicing alcoholics, many of us drank to medicate our pain in the first place, so it follows that if in the process of recovery we only continue to repress or deny these feelings, then emotional sobriety would be made impossible. After all, using some kind of medication was all many of us understood when it came to dealing with emotional pain, conflict and anxiety. All the while a great truth remained hidden and unacknowledged:

Sobriety in the fullest sense means regaining our sanity by recovering our emotional lives.

The adult child struggle, the co-dependency struggle, involves a crazy and insane lifestyle in which we continue to fail at life because we continue to follow the rules which deny us the permission to be ourselves. Working our program means more than just looking or acting "as if" — more than going through the motions.

Going through the motions in the beginning may help, but long-term recovery means building a recovery program from the inside out. To do otherwise is to remain "Lost in the Shuffle." That's the simple truth, and it's the reason why the co-dependent gets so damned anxious when they start to break through their denial and all the issues that surround them. Co-dependents, as I've pointed out before, love to throw up distractions, side issues — the kids, the job, the spouse, the money . . . anything to stay out of touch with themselves. Anything to avoid painful self-analysis.

That's what the co-dependent's identity struggle is really all about, getting back to the self, letting go of all the hype, and starting to build from the inside out. Real recovery means putting it back together inside by forming a trusting relationship with ourselves. Hanging on to the old ways, the old issues, and the old rules only serves to perpetuate the co-dependents' separation from themselves.

So, then, where do we start?

The whole purpose of recovery is that you and I would become whole people, and if we are to do this — if we are to become whole — then we must begin *where we are*. We must recognize that recovery, above all, is a *process* and that there is no singular point of arrival, no final destination, only the process of facing each day together with ourselves.

Co-dependents don't like this notion of having to start from where they are. They've spent a lot of time and energy staying out of touch with their feelings, out of touch with their inner selves. Obviously if they really liked where they were, there would be no need for change in the first place. But they don't want to be where they are. They really want to experience all the benefits of recovery without having to go through the process. They want to get someplace other than where they are without having to own the responsibility of change.

Co-dependents have a child's fear, fear of the dark and of the terrible demons that lurk on the other side of change.

Co-dependents need a healthy adult and parent model to walk them through their fear and demonstrate for them that these terrible demons of change can't destroy them. In large part, this is the role of the therapist in treatment for co-dependency. I've never met an effective therapist working with adult children who didn't recognize this basic need in their co-dependent clients . . . the need for a healthy role model.

Yet strangely enough this simple philosophy is often overlooked in the process of treatment.

I believe that if a counselor can be a good parent, a good guide and a patient mentor, then the client will ultimately begin to move in the direction they need to go — toward a sane and healthy relationship with themselves. There are many roads to the top of the mountain, but the summit is always the same — we're all trying to get back to a place where we can be at peace with ourselves.

True identity lies behind the individual's pseudo-identity that is reflected in what they do for a job, how much money they make, what religion they are, who they know, or where they live.

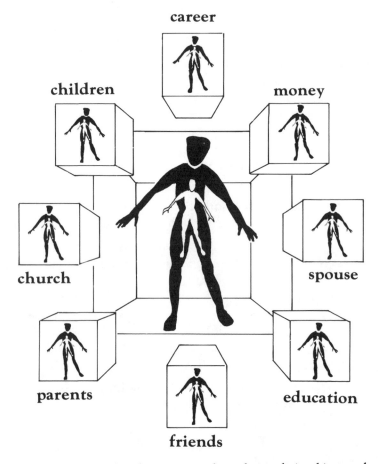

career

children money

church spouse

parents education

friends

Recovery means breaking our co-dependent relationship on the outside issues so we can get back to ourselves.

The Importance of Support

So in recovery we need to find a mentor, a sponsor, or perhaps a group who will walk with us and lend support through the often-difficult process of recovery.

An excerpt from a letter I received from one of my recovering co-dependent clients illustrates this need for direction and support in recovery:

Recovery has been a difficult process. The more I get into it, the more I remember. I continue on because I have made a commitment to myself and to the process. I believe that recovery is a lifetime journey and I am traveling at my own speed. I feel great sorrow when those I love choose not to break out of the hurtful co-dependent patterns that we once shared together. I can only continue on my path and hope that someday they may join me. I now accept my need for help as well as complete responsibility for myself and my choices. I swear to God that I will no longer abandon myself. God help me to grow in kindness, patience and gentleness with myself.

When you have an infection, the pain is always there until you open the wound and drain out the poison. I am beginning to do just that, as difficult a process as this has been, I am also beginning to feel much better. I feel more peace in my heart than I have ever felt before. I feel like I'm beginning to release my stranglehold on life. I'm starting to slow down, to begin to learn what it means to relax — to be at rest. I'm beginning to feel at peace with myself. I don't have to run and hide the truth anymore, or to keep myself so occupied that I won't think about my frightening past. No more secrets — now I can begin to be quietly with myself, I can rest. I don't have to be so afraid anymore.

I feel like I've had major surgery. It feels like I took up a sharp knife and made a very painful incision into my heart. But it was necessary to let out the infection. I have felt poison slowly draining, oozing out of the incision, and when

*it is done draining, I will wash the wound clean, sew the
torn edges together . . . and I will heal.*

*Thank you, Bob, for being my guide and for believing in
me. Thank you for your tears as I faced the darkest corner
of my past. They were more validating than any words you
could have spoken. Alone I would have never opened the
door. I needed to take the risk to share with someone else
and trust them to be there for me. Now I trust in myself to be
there for me as well.*

Yours truly,
Judy D.

You see, the real danger in recovery for the co-dependent
is the choice to continue to do it alone. Remaining alone is
almost always a set-up to get lost in the shuffle. Alone we
are unable to resolve our conflicts and as a result we begin
again to look for the quick fix or some medication to ease
the burden.

There is no short-cut, and as they say, the shortest distance between two points is a straight line. For co-dependents this means letting go of all the issues, one by one.
Work, school, drugs, food, relationships — you need to
disengage from all of the things that can sabotage your recovery. In fact, the process of recovery cannot truly begin
until you've abandoned your addictions.

(In passing, I should mention that I've never seen a spontaneous recovery from co-dependency. As I've said before, it
takes time. How much time? Well, that depends on a lot of
factors, like how long you've been caught up in the game,
how much support you have to change, and how motivated
you are. Generally speaking, however, a minimum of three
to five years wouldn't be unrealistic.)

While I believe that getting off our drug (or issue) of
choice is the first step in recovery from co-dependency, I
don't believe that simple abstinence is any guarantee of recovery. Similarly, I don't believe that co-dependency itself

is an issue unique to alcoholics or to those who have grown up with or who have married an alcoholic.

When I first began to think about co-dependency this way, I got a lot of flack from my colleagues because co-dependency was viewed as an issue that affected only those who lived with an alcoholic. Before that we affectionately referred to the co-dependent as a significant other, or S.O.B.'s for short. The earliest reference to the co-dependent population was simply the "affected."

But those who spoke glibly of co-dependency early on just weren't saying very much about how this condition called co-dependency was transmitted from an alcoholic's struggle with alcoholism into some other kind of strange and unique illness or dysfunction that the people who were living with that alcoholic were now displaying.

Despite the fact that I had come from an alcoholic family, I wasn't talking about myself — at that time, I was just an alcoholic. While I understood that co-dependency was somehow linked to the alcoholic experience, it took some time for me to recognize that I too was a co-dependent. Today I see co-dependency as an underlying fabric in the lives of many people, and not just those who are alcoholic or who came from an alcoholic family. Coming to this new understanding of co-dependency and its importance in the process of recovery meant expanding the boundaries of my program to include powerlessness and unmanageability over lots of other things, like work, food, and relationships, to name a few.

So back then, I assumed that life was going to get better just by not drinking. I also assumed that if I quit drinking things would get better for those, you know, *co-dependent* folks around me.

I counted on that, but it seemed like the longer I stayed sober, the worse I felt. I didn't get happier in sobriety, I got more depressed and anxious. This really bothered me. What if the craziness inside wasn't just the result of my drinking? Maybe I really was a nut. I started to think about things that I had never thought about or felt before — not even during the worst of my drinking.

By two years into my sobriety, when by all rights I should have been getting some of that fabled serenity, I was instead beginning to think that I was a Class A certifiable nut.

This was a cruel twist because in the beginning of my recovery from alcoholism, I had heard and believed that all my troubles were due to my alcoholism, and not insanity. I was an alcoholic who felt crazy because of his drinking and not a crazy person who was drinking to deal with his craziness. Or so the logic suggested.

Now, however, a strange thing happened. I was not drinking, but I was acting as though I were. Was I on a "Dry Drunk?" That's how we labelled flaming co-dependency back then.

One thing is certain: I seemed to be getting worse instead of better. I started feeling angry, but I didn't know why. I started fighting with people over things that didn't make any sense. I worried about what other people were thinking about me. I was paranoid.

I started thinking about quitting my job and breaking up with my girlfriend. I thought a lot about getting drunk or worse—committing suicide. "Life's a bitch, and then you die," I morosely repeated to myself.

My old *drinking* friends said things like, "Bob, you sure were easier to live with when you were drinking." Or: "That AA program of yours is making you sick."

On the other side my AA friends were saying, "Bob, you just aren't working your program."

What was I really doing? Was I fighting with windmills, or was there something more to sobriety than simply not drinking?

Chapter 16

Abstinence and Beyond

Inside recovery I began asking myself, "What is there beyond not drinking? If this is all there is, then I don't know how long I'm going to hang on."

In my AA family there was a long tradition of KISS — Keep It Simple, Stupid. I understood all that and worked the program. That's how it went: Read the book, go to meetings, don't drink, let go — all those other slogans that are so much a part of the AA Fellowship.

That's great stuff, truly great stuff. I don't question the wisdom of it at all. I'm a loyal recovering member of AA. But I know that AA is a family. And I know that, in theory, families must mature. I also know that, in theory again, individuals must mature across a predictable course over time. And I reason that families and culture must likewise mature across time.

My AA family had matured to the point of understanding very clearly the KISS philosophy that helped us focus on and address the issue of not drinking as a first step toward regaining sanity in our lives. So once I started getting my sobriety down and wasn't thinking about drinking every ten minutes or being preoccupied about how I was going to make it sober through the next New Year's Eve celebration that was still 11 months away . . . I wondered what was next.

And so it is with many co-dependents in recovery. Once we go past the initial stages of getting off our drugs of choice, letting go and working our programs, what we often feel is an emerging sense of anxiety — anxiety that has no clear connection with our drinking, our over-eating, our workaholism, or our preoccupation with others. Our anxiety is a free-floating anxiety linked to a troubled past of unresolved issues, such as physical, emotional or psychological abuse, abandonment or neglect.

It's important to stress once again that there are lots of people in the world, not just individuals from alcoholic homes or alcoholic marriages who reflect the characteristics of co-dependency. These same characteristics, these same coping patterns may be seen in people who come from a variety of troubled family histories.

The commonalities also show up in:

1. Emotionally and chronically mentally ill family systems
2. Physically or sexually abusive family systems
3. Rigid fundamentalistic family systems

What these systems have in common with the alcoholic family is that the dysfunctional rules of these systems deny the individual the freedom to be who they really are. The systems are oppressive and constricting. Children living under the dysfunctional rules of a troubled family are forced to grow up in a hurried fashion and take on prematurely the responsibilities of adulthood in order to take care of themselves and their sick family.

If we came from such a family system we not only got lost in the shuffle as children, we were destined to remain lost as adults, spouses, parents, and friends. We were destined to fail, not because we were bad people, but because we didn't know who we were.

In recovery the delayed identity of our past and the innate drive to explore and find ourselves begins to take hold again . . . picking up wherever we left off. There's no simple way to describe this process. The best I've come up with is an Eastern philosophy that says, "To be at peace, one must learn to live in the question."

Living in the question is a real challenge for most co-dependents because it runs totally opposite to everything they've learned about survival, things like: Don't ever be lost, always know where you're going, never let anybody know how you're really feeling, be strong and always, always be in control . . . of everything.

I discovered in the process of my own recovery that the greatest anxiety I felt came from trying to be in control all the time. When the shit was hitting the fan, I stood there like nothing was happening. This was confusing to people around me because their reality never seemed to match my reality. I must have looked crazy to them. They'd say, "Don't you understand what's going on? Can't you see what's happening?"

And I'd say casually, "Sure, I understand, but things are fine, everything's going to be okay. I've been in worse situations." Being in a crisis felt normal and looking good was a part of the game. On the inside, though, I'd be thinking, "Oh Christ, if they could just see what's going on with me, they'd send me to the looney bin."

Why did I believe that it was always my job to be in control of everything, other people, or situations (which I really had no power over in the first place)? Where did I come up with that private logic that this was what I was supposed to do?

Who taught me how to do this? Certainly I wasn't born with this need to control everything, to play God. Being God, of course, can be a very lonely ordeal.

Now I don't believe that you and I were meant to end up thinking or feeling this way about life. But co-dependents often have a family history that says to them . . . it's not OK for you to do the things you need to do in order to become a whole person.

And that's what recovery is all about. Finding yourself and finding out that you have a choice. As I've mentioned before, the adult child and the co-dependent don't achieve a clear sense of themselves for some very specific reasons.

The chemically dependent person is no exception: Beyond sobriety there is still recovery from co-dependency.

Years ago AA co-founder Bill Wilson had, through his own recovery, begun to recognize this second stage in sobriety. Imbued with divine understanding, Bill Wilson late in his career spoke of it this way, "The challenge for the AA program over the next century is to help its membership recover their emotional lives."

From his own unique perspective, I believe he was talking about co-dependency and the pursuit of emotional recovery within the ranks of Alcoholics Anonymous. I believe he understood the hidden potential of the Twelve Steps to lead its membership through the confusion, isolation, and emotional despair of a troubled co-dependent history. Given the time, I believe that Bill W. would have continued to support the cause of emotional sobriety as a part of the grander mission in both AA and Al-Anon.

If you ask me, the Twelve Steps of AA are still the best treatment program for co-dependents.

Are AA and Al-Anon necessarily made up right now of a membership that knows how to do this?

No.

Will they be?

Yes.

But, the question arises: "How will that happen if no one wants to risk the conflict of change as regards the application of the Twelve Step program?" After all, adult children are raised in a situation where they don't want any conflict. Conflict rocks the boat. Conflict sets one up for pain, rejection and abandonment.

So we learn to become skilled at manipulating and lying to avoid conflict. You've got to know a lot about conflict and truth in order to avoid it. Someone who always manages to side-step the truth is someone who knows a lot about it. We co-dependents know a lot about it because we've built a career out of making sure that we didn't step in it. In reality our lying doesn't really protect us, instead it makes us vulnerable.

Does this seem paradoxical? Well it is but recovery from co-dependency is filled with little paradoxes.

The Bowling Ball Paradox: A Paradigm

My image of a co-dependent's life goes something like this: They're trying to swim the English channel with a bowling ball in their hand and no one is there to help them. Somehow they manage to keep their head above water and suck in just enough air to stay afloat. Determined to make it the hard way, one breath at a time.

Now, it just so happens that there are also healthy folks trying to cross the channel, but they're using a boat with two oars and a bailing bucket. Sometime these healthy mariners catch sight of a floundering co-dependent and guided by compassion they feel compelled to row over and offer their help.

They begin their conversation with the drowning co-dependent by saying: "I notice from a distance that you look to be in a bit of distress."

Going down for the third time, the co-dependent gasps back in a gurgling voice, "I'm fine. What makes you think I need any help?"

This is a very confusing and disconcerting message to the person in the boat. But these good Samaritans are persistent folks. So they row around to the other side just to take one more look. Seeing the bowling ball in the co-dependent's hand convinces the good Samaritan that things are really not okay. Meanwhile, the co-dependent becomes increasingly agitated over the intrusion of this unwanted helper.

Having recognized the bowling ball as the source of the problem, the person in the boat is compelled yet again to confront the situation . . . "No wonder you're having trouble," they say. "Do you know you've got a bowling ball in your hand?"

The adult child indignantly snaps back, "Yeah, so what? It's my bowling ball. It's the only bowling ball I've ever owned."

The adult child continues, "In fact, this bowling ball belonged to my mother's mother's *mother's* . . . *mother.* It's been in our family for generations and I'm not going to be the one to drop the ball."

The healthy person says, "Well, I was going to suggest that you let go of it, but under the circumstances, maybe you'd better not." Now, you see, even the healthy person can get sucked in — seduced by the craziness of such a game. "Just hang on to the side of my boat," they tell the co-dependent, "and I'll row you to safety."

"So," the co-dependent says, "You just can't mind your own business, can you? Well, maybe this will help you get the point."

With that, the co-dependent throws his arm up over his head along with the bowling ball in his hand and drops it right through the bottom of the healthy person's boat. Now, while the newly drenched, once healthy person is trying to save himself, the co-dependent turns to him and says: "Well, if you have to be here, the least you could do is help me carry this damn bowling ball."

Ironic, isn't it, that the helper in this story ends up getting soaked. What a paradox! Sometimes, staying healthy means rowing away from those who can't or won't accept help.

Recovery, as I mentioned, is also a paradox: You need to become dependent in order to become independent, you need to surrender control in order to gain it and you need to embrace the past in order to face the future. For the recovering co-dependent I believe these paradoxical truths are basic to the process of change and central to our search for identity.

Learning to give up the bowling ball of dysfunctional rules and face the anxiety of change is the first step in our co-dependent recovery. By casting aside the rules of our co-dependent past we can begin again to grow and develop as human beings, remembering always that the true gift of recovery lies in the process of being true to yourself and thereby finding a clear identity.

Chapter 17

Recovery Hints and Reminders

DON'T STOP NOW!! If you found yourself identifying with the examples or the concepts presented thus far in *LOST IN THE SHUFFLE*, then you might want to consider a couple of questions:

1. Do you want to change?
2. Are you ready to change?

Sometimes it's hard to answer these questions directly with a firm and self-assured "Yes! I want to change and, by God, I'm ready!" Or: "No, I don't think I need to change."

Do you have a feeling of fear and excitement over the very idea of change? These seemingly incompatible emotions in combination are, in my experience, an indication of a desire, willingness and need to make a change.

For those who have come this far and feel a tinge of excitement and fear over the prospect of change, I have put together a list of hints and reminders to help you begin a process of recovery.

Hints and Reminders

1. Take one thing at a time. Recovery is a process that begins by starting where you are and by taking care of first things first. If you are an alcoholic, a bulimic, an anorexic, a workaholic, a gambling addict, an over-

eater, or a relationship addict, then start by getting help to take care of that issue first. *Take time to end the addiction.* Take time to get off your primary drug of choice. How long will it take? Perhaps one or two years, but remember: These will not be years spent in drudgery and self-denial, but they will be years filled with learning a new way of life, building healthy relationships and laying the foundation for self-actualization.

2. Remember that no one recovers alone from co-dependency. If you are isolated and have no support system, then you must take steps to seek one out. Find a counselor, a therapy group or a self-help program that can help you find your way out of dependency and co-dependency.

3. Stay with your new-found support system. Be consistent and tenacious about calling on them for help.

4. Focus on building trust in others' ability to help you. Trusting relationships are essential to facing the many risks of change. Trust them and you will begin to trust in yourself.

5. Move at a pace that you feel comfortable with. This means you don't have to do everything according to some ideal schedule of recovery. It means that you don't have to do everything at once. This does not mean writing your own program, but simply means taking on only what you believe you can handle, given your resources. Your support system would be an excellent place to check out how realistic you are being about change. Recovery does not happen like a lightning bolt. Recovery is a process, and takes place in increments over time.

6. You have the right to say "No." If it feels like the wrong thing to do, don't do it. This is *your* recovery, not someone else's. So when in doubt, check it out. Healthy systems of support will allow you the time and offer you the opportunity to prepare for change.

7. Put yourself first on the list of people to consider in the

process of change. This does not give license to ignore the needs of others, but serves as a reminder to be, above all, considerate to yourself. Again, your support network will help you make decisions in a balanced and caring way. Let them help you explore the options.

8. Change often makes others react with hurt, fear, anger and resentment. You are part of a system and when you change, it puts strain on the system — others feel the stress. But remember that you are responsible to yourself first and others second. You can care about them without having to take care of them. Children may be the greatest challenge for you to face in this respect.

9. Take time to celebrate your successes, no matter how small.

10. Put more energy into loving yourself than you do in trying to love others. Learning how to love yourself is at the heart of learning how to love others in a healthy way.

11. Your feelings are okay — your reaction to them may *not* be. Learn to make this distinction. Healthy systems of support will validate your feelings and will offer you guidance on how to constructively deal with them.

12. No one recovers perfectly. Human beings sometimes make mistakes and fail. Healthy systems of support allow for mistakes.

13. Never take more than 50 percent of the responsibility in any relationship with other adults.

14. Try to avoid focusing on the problems of others and try to avoid solving their problems for them. Don't waste time taking their inventories, mulling over their moral lapses and making tallies of their undesirable traits.

15. When you don't know the answer to something, admit that you don't know. When you want to know the answer, if there is one, ask someone who does know. And when you need help to do something, ask for it.

16. Don't assume that others understand or care about what you want or need.

17. Remember to take time to rest and play.
18. Eat when you feel hungry, and sleep when you feel tired.
19. Share your feelings and problems in a safe place. Grieve your losses, but don't grieve interminably — don't become defined by your grief and dependent upon it. And be as understanding with yourself as you are with others.
20. Be true to yourself, above all, and remember wherever you go, there you will be.

Recovery Exercises

- For starters, pick any one of the 20 hints I just listed, write it down on a three by five card, take it with you every day for a month, and several times a day (at specific times, if possible), take the card out and read it. Do this for a month with each of the 20 hints, and you will have demonstrated to yourself, if to no one else, your ability to make a commitment and see it through. Whatever else you may learn as a result of this exercise rests in the process of doing it.

- Writing in a journal every couple of days or so is another simple way to begin to invest yourself in change. I have found that many of the co-dependents I've worked with in recovery have found that keeping a journal was a productive exercise.

  I have used a journal in my own recovery and noted at the beginning there were many things I would not have said out loud to myself or to anyone else. Writing these things down was my first real experience with breaking the silence of the "no talk" rules in my family history. I wrote about my relationships, my family, my feelings, my hopes and my dreams. I wrote letters to myself and to the little boy in me. I wrote letters to my inner adult and parent. I wrote letters to my father, my mother, my sisters and my brother.

  After a year or two of journal writing, I started to see

certain patterns in my thinking, and I began to acknowledge some of the feelings I had inside. Eventually, I shared many of the things I wrote about with my recovering friends.

The healing process cannot be hurried, but at least my writing didn't stop it from happening. I encourage you to seriously consider this option.

JOURNALING IN RECOVERY

To help demonstrate further the value of *journaling in recovery*, I have included several entries selected from a journal written by Judy, a recovering client of mine. In allowing me to use this material, Judy expressed the hope that her sharing would be of help to other recovering co-dependents who read her journal entries.

Excerpts from Judy's Journal

March, 1986
    . . . *When I was one year old, my father began to be violent. He got angry and smashed up a chair. My brother Vince, age two, cowered in a corner, quivering and shaking in fear. FEAR is really how I can best describe my childhood. I have blocked out most of my recollection of events, but I have a clear sense that the over-riding emotion was FEAR. I remember always being afraid — afraid of my father. He was explosive and unpredictable. I think that his unpredictability was what made him most frightening to me. He was like Dr. Jekyll and Mr. Hyde.*

One moment sweet and smiling, and the next moment, for no apparent reason — at the drop of a hat — the expression on his face would change to one of rage, twisted and contorted in anger. WHY? There was never any way to anticipate the next explosion or to prevent it. I spent my whole life walking on eggshells, filled with anxiety and dread, waiting for the next explosion, trying to hide from his rage, trying to escape, to get out of the way of the fallout.

. . . *My stomach was always in a knot. I could never feel relaxed or at ease around my father. My adrenalin level was always high, like a runner waiting for the start of the race for the gun to go off and to start running. I was always poised for the "fight or flight" response to fear — but for me it was always flight. He had more ways than one to frighten us, it wasn't just the fear of being beaten. He would scream and shout, his angry face was frightening. He would break and smash things. The anticipation was terrible. He'd smash his fist through a wall —would I be next? I must have used enough adrenalin for ten people in my lifetime. Right now I am so tense just remembering that my body aches from head to toe. My muscles are in painful knots, it's hard to breathe . . .*

April, 1986

. . . *My father physically and sexually abused my older sister more than any of us. In her adulthood, Kathy has told me that she felt angry at me because I "got off easier" than she did . . . IT WAS NOT EASIER . . . It was horrifying to stand helplessly by and witness her abuse, or that of my other sister, or more rarely, my brother. I felt enormous guilt and anguish whenever it was Kathy being hurt instead of me, I felt every blow emotionally just as surely as she felt them physically. I feel nauseated — sick to my stomach with outrage, helplessness, sorrow, and grief. IT IS WRONG TO HURT CHILDREN . . . IT IS WRONG TO HURT PEOPLE!*

Whenever my sister was beaten, I stood stiff with fear, grateful that it wasn't me, but afraid that at any moment he would turn on me. I scarcely dared to draw a breath. I remember my father sitting on top of my sister pinning her down, his leather strap raised to hit her, asking her where she wanted the welts this time — she had to pick. It makes me sick. My mother was there watching. SHE NEVER PROTECTED US FROM HIM . . . She never tried to stop him, she never tried to help us. I wished with all my heart that my mother would take us away, would divorce him. She eventually did after 30 years, but by then I was married and a parent myself . . .

May, 1986

. . . Once I was standing at the kitchen sink washing dishes. My father came up quietly behind me and without a word, hit me a hard blow. (I learned later he was angry about something I had accidentally broken in the past.) His sneak attack had a profound effect on me. Although my trust level was already very low — it was at that point that my ability or willingness to trust shut down completely. I became absolutely convinced that I could never let my guard down for a minute. I was always tensed, wincing, waiting for the next blow. Why did I get hit when I had done nothing wrong? It was then that I began to feel totally hopeless. Life was not meant to be good. Life could not be good for me. "Life is not a bed of roses" was my motto. I always expected thorns. If my own father would turn on me and sneak up on me and hit me without warning — if my own mother would not protect me from him — then WHO would help, WHO would care about me, WHO would acknowledge that this was wrong? Our family doctor was silent, neighbors hearing shouts and cries never said a word, and relatives never questioned. I felt so small, so alone, so helpless. I gave up hoping then that anyone would ever care that I was hurt, that anyone would ever help me or tell me that I deserved better, that IT IS WRONG TO HURT CHILDREN . . .

. . . The worst abandonment of all was that I gave up on myself too. I've come to the realization that although my child's fear originated with my father, my real fear now is of me. I was struck with the clear realization that I have abandoned myself. There have been times in the past when I felt my life was so hopeless, discouraged and depressed that I felt my life was worthless. It's no wonder that the "child within me" has always run around in absolute panic and fear because I thought her worthless, not worthy of protection or care or concern. I was horrified and heartsick when I realized this, and I wept in sorrow and grief . . .

. . . I always felt so alone, so afraid. I must have determined early that I would survive on my own, and I set about using my creativity to do so. I figured that if I made myself invisible — if I escaped notice — to that degree I would escape physical abuse. I *lived my life in isolation, withdrawn from other people, because I learned early that I certainly couldn't trust. I imagined myself so invisible that I could hide behind the wallpaper. I imagined myself non-existent. I was very quiet. I never rocked the boat or drew attention to myself. I knew intuitively what behaviors would anger my father and set him off, and I avoided them like the plague. But the irony is that I didn't escape at all . . . My father's rages were so inconsistent and illogical, that try though I might, I could never control them. When I escaped being physically or sexually abused more often than my sisters, I wasn't any better off. The awful anxiety of anticipating being hurt at any time for no reason, and the heartsickness I felt at witnessing my sisters' actual abuse, and the guilt I felt for escaping . . . all combined to cause me to suffer as greatly as anyone else in my family. Emotional wounds are every bit as grievous as physical wounds.*

June, 1986

. . . My two sisters and I shared a room, and I shared a bed with one of my sisters. We were not allowed to close our bedroom door because my father said he might want us to do something, and if the door was shut, we wouldn't hear him call. The lack of privacy in our home devastated me. I felt so invaded and spied-on — never safe. Once when he was angry, he removed the door from the bathroom. I was about thirteen at the time and would struggle to wrap the shower curtain around myself to use the toilet . . .

. . . My father was sexually abusive as well. He raped my sister when she was fifteen. She kept it a secret until she was an adult and then she told me and our mother. My mother said she didn't believe her. "He wouldn't do THAT!" I never doubted my sister for a minute. I have really uneasy feelings about my father as a lecherous man. Just the look on his face made my skin crawl. Sometimes, something will remind me of my father and my skin actually hurts to be touched. My father used to fondle my sister's breasts and then pretend it was an accident, like he thought it was my mother. Sometimes my father would expose himself, once to my sister and her friend, and I remember walking past the

bathroom door when I was twelve or thirteen and seeing my father naked with an erection, brushing his teeth. It was a sickening jolt. He would say we couldn't tell my mom anything because it would make her sick . . .

. . . We were supposed to keep quiet and not complain because my mother always said, "Blessed are the peacemakers, for they shall be called children of God . . ." My father had a fetish about honesty. He would rant and rave about how severely we would be punished whenever we got caught telling a lie. That put us in a difficult position — if we told the truth, we risked an explosion because it was something that would make him mad. If we got caught in a lie, it would be even worse. The irony was that he lived a lie himself . . .

. . . My lack of trust carried through to my adulthood. I locked everything up tight, trying to be safe from harm. I locked the backyard gates, I locked the upstairs' storage rooms, I locked the freezer in the basement. I always kept the doors to the house locked, never leaving them open for a minute. And most importantly, I kept my upstairs' study locked. And I didn't feel safe. I felt more vulnerable than ever. I wouldn't even vacuum a rug with my back to the door, I was so convinced of the harm that would come to me . . .

July, 1986

. . . After I was married, each of my parents told me that the other one didn't love me. My father said, "Your mother only loved babies. Once you were past the baby stage, she didn't love you."

My mother said, "You know, your father never loved you."

. . . Ten months before my father's death, I talked to him for the last time. He called me up and began talking normally. He became increasingly agitated and expressed great anger and bitterness that I wouldn't let him see my sons. (I had stopped seeing him several years earlier, but he continued to call me once in a while.) He kept asking me for help and I kept repeating, "I can't help you — you need professional help!"

He'd say, "If you can't count on your family, who can you count on?" He began to scream at me, swearing and shouting. He *screamed, "You're BAD! You're as BAD as your God-damned mother!"*

I hung up . . . Those were the last words from my father.

. . . After he died, I received a copy of his will. He named me, not even spelling my name right, and stated, "It is my express desire and intention to disinherit my daughters and any of their children."

I want to thank Judy for her courage and willingness to share these excerpts from her recovery journal.

- Another useful technique in recovery and self-analysis is in the making of a collage of your family story, your childhood and your role in it. This is not an art project, and there is no right or wrong way to do it. No grade will be given. All that is expected in this collage exercise is a willingness on your part to see it through. The purpose of this exercise is to gain insight and understanding of ourselves, our history and our feelings.

    To begin a collage of your own, simply set some time aside (usually no less than about six hours), sit down with a piece of poster board (about 20″ by 20″), a family photo album, a variety of magazines (*Time*, *Newsweek*, *Vogue*, *Cosmo*, *People*, etc.), a good pair of scissors, some glue or paste, color crayons, an ink pen, or even watercolors and put together a collage of images, colors, words, drawings, and pictures that reflect the feelings, thoughts and recollections of your troubled family history. Try to include some image or photo of yourself as a child.

    This exercise works best if you share your collage with a therapist, a support group or someone you trust. It helps to get feedback about the contrast or congruence between the collage and how others see you. No matter how you do this exercise, it will help you start building a relationship with yourself. I have made several collages of my own over the past six years just to help me stay in touch with myself and my progress.

Like keeping a journal, this exercise can help monitor your progress in recovery.

Doing a collage of your past may be a painful experience, but the healing process often begins this way. Believe in yourself and know that to embrace your past is a necessary step in the process of healing.

- Search through a family photo album and pick out two or three pictures of yourself as a child. Try to select pictures that speak to your intuitive image of how you felt as a child. Trust me, you'll know which ones are right when you see them. If you don't have any family photos, this in itself will tell you something about your history.

  Once you've found the picture that best reflects the child within you, put it up on the bathroom mirror or someplace else where you can see it every day. Put a copy in your wallet or your purse. (You keep photos of the other important people in your life, don't you?)

- A final exercise that I would recommend is this: Take at least one hour a week to be totally alone with yourself. Time to just be, to reflect, to feel, to meditate or pray. No books, no TV, no radio, no hubbub. Be with yourself. While you are doing this, focus your thoughts on changing one of the rules which you believe is keeping you locked into a co-dependent life. Take one rule every month, and for each day of that month, modify, temper or break the rule altogether. This does not mean that you now have license to become an outlaw. But it means that you will take the time to reflect on the dysfunctional rules that guided your development, and that you will give yourself permission to find alternatives to those rules.

A CLOSING NOTE

Behind the pages of any book worth writing I believe there must be a purpose. It is my hope that *LOST IN THE SHUFFLE* has in some way advanced the purpose for which it was written — recovery from co-dependency and the development of a clear identity.

Professional Care.
Professional Concern.
Professional Counselor . . .
just for you!

Brought to you by Health Communications, Inc., *Professional Counselor* is dedicated to serving the addictions and mental health fields. With Richard Fields, Ph.D., an authority in Dual Diagnosis, serving as editor, and in-depth articles and columns written by and for professionals, you will get the timely information you need to best serve your clients. *Professional Counselor*'s coverage includes:

- Treatment advances
- Mental health and addictions research
- Family, group and special populations therapy
- The latest in counseling techniques
- Listing of upcoming workshops and events
- Managed care and employee assistance programs

Professional Counselor: Serving the Addictions and Mental Health Fields is <u>the</u> magazine for counselors, therapists, addictionologists, psychologists, managed-care specialists and employee assistance program personnel.

Order *Professional Counselor* today and take advantage of our special introductory offer: One year of *Professional Counselor* (6 bimonthy issues) for just $20.00. That's 23% off the regular subscription price!

Clip and mail to:
Professional Counselor, P.O. Box 607, Mount Morris, IL 61054-7641

YES! Enter my subscription to *Professional Counselor* for a full year (6 bimonthly issues) for only $20.00—23% off the regular subscription price. If you are not completely satisfied, simply return the subscription invoice marked CANCEL. The first issue will be yours to keep.

Name: _____

Address: _____

City: _____ State: _____ Zip: _____

☐ Payment enclosed   Charge my: ☐ Visa ☐ MC

_____ Exp.: _____

Signature: _____

Please allow 4-6 weeks for delivery. FL residents please add $1.20 state sales tax.